Turn Left

Turn Left

Spinning an Intercultural Identity

Illah Nourbakhsh

SENTIENT PUBLICATIONS

A paperback original
Cover design by Laura Johanna Waltje
Book design by Laura Johanna Waltje

Publisher's Cataloging-in-Publication Data

Names: Nourbakhsh, Illah R., author.
Title: Turn left : Spinning an Intercultural Identity / Illah Nourbakhsh.
Description: Boulder, CO: Sentient Publications, 2025.
Identifiers: LCCN: 2024949581 | ISBN: 9781591813187 (paperback) | 9781591813194 (epub)
Subjects: LCSH Nourbakhsh, Illah R. | Iranian Americans--Biography.
| Iranians--United States--Biography. | Immigrants--Biography. |
Scientists--Biography. | Educators--Biography. | BISAC BIOGRAPHY &
AUTOBIOGRAPHY / Memoirs | BIOGRAPHY & AUTOBIOGRAPHY
/ Science & Technology | BIOGRAPHY & AUTOBIOGRAPHY / Arab &
Middle Eastern
Classification: LCC E184.I5 .N68 2025 | DDC 305.89155/092--dc23

SENTIENT PUBLICATIONS
A Limited Liability Company
PO Box 1851
Boulder, CO 80306
www.sentientpublications.com

To all immigrants

Advance Praise for
Turn Left

"Not only is Illah Nourbakhsh's *Turn Left* a crisply written, witty and insightful tale of migration to the United States, it is simultaneously about the possibilities and limits of technology from someone who's curiosity has been as vast as his impact. If the relationship between immigration and technological innovation in America isn't already clear, then let this be the text that renders that relationship canonical."

Louis Chude-Sokei
Professor of English, George and Joyce Wein Chair, Boston University
Director of African-American and Black Diaspora Studies

"*Turn Left* is a searching and powerful exploration of what it means to operate in the "in between" spaces of modern America and our changing world. In a memoir that is both deeply personal and accessibly universal, Illah Nourbakhsh describes what it is like to navigate these times as an immigrant, an Iranian-born American, and as a technologist battling the social disequilibrium that his own profession has helped cause. As revealed in this touching account, he is that rare roboticist and computer scientist who is as interested in social dynamics as he is in technology. His exquisite understanding of power, narratives, and what our communities truly thirst for should make this book required reading for anyone trying to bridge the gap between our large institutions and our neighborhoods where community finds its home. If the world feels out of control today, *Turn Left* offers an unpretentious path through the madness rooted in the simplest and most promising of formulas—seeing and hearing each other in new and more profound ways."

Grant Oliphant
CEO, Conrad Prebys Foundation

"With Iran being a US foe for about 45 years, it is easy to fail to think of the humanity of Iranians. This moving book about an Iranian immigrant to the US reminds the American reader of our shared humanity. Illah Nourbakhsh tells the touching story of a young Iranian boy who immigrated to the US, became a professor of robotics in one of the best computer-science departments in the world, and has decided to dedicate his career not to the betterment of technology, but for the betterment of the world. It is a story that makes me hopeful not only about America but also about the Middle East."

Moshe Vardi
University Professor and George Distinguished Service Professor in Computational Engineering, Rice University

"I thought I knew and liked Illah, but *Turn Left* gave me an incredible perspective about what it's like to immigrate to the US, be caught between two cultures, guided by curiosity and an extreme desire to make the world a better place. Absolutely inspiring!"

Alan Eustace

"*Turn Left* by Illah Nourbakhsh is a heartwarming yet honest reflection on the experience of growing up as a migrant in the United States. Through candid narration, Nourbakhsh shares the complexities of trying to fit into a new culture while striving to preserve his own identity. The book is filled with moments of introspection and decision-making, where the author is driven by the desire to retain his values and create positive outcomes in a world full of challenges. With each "turn left" moment, Nourbakhsh reminds us that we, too, encounter pivotal choices in life, and through perseverance and authenticity, we can overcome obstacles and make meaningful contributions to the world. This beautifully told personal journey serves as a powerful reminder of resilience and the impact one can have despite life's difficulties."

Prof. Tan Sri Dr Jemilah Mahmood
Executive Director
Sunway Centre for Planetary Health, Sunway University Malaysia

Contents

Foreword

November, 1953. Dwight D. Eisenhower is President of the United States. Robert F. Wagner (pronounced Wag-ner, as in the movement of a dog's tail, "not Vahg-ner, Mummy") is Mayor of New York City. And I am sitting in study hall with other members of the freshman class of the McBurney School for boys on 63rd Street, just off Central Park West.

Silence.

"Please, sir." The accent is unmistakably not American. "Does anyone heeaah (practically a three-syllable word) have a rubber?"

My parents were refugees from Germany to England in the late 1930s. I was born in England and am, on that day, a very recent, thirteen-year-old immigrant to the United States. Immigrant, not refugee. There's a distinction. Although for the moment, it is totally irrelevant. I have a very distinctive English accent. And I do not yet speak American. I speak English; and in England, a rubber is an eraser. In New York, judging by the wave of uproarious laughter, it clearly is not. Eventually, (my memory is slightly foggy on the details) I come to understand that I have just asked for a condom. Welcome to America.

Some years earlier, during the war, General George Patton had amused an English audience by observing that Great Britain and the United States were two great countries separated by a common language. Where was General Patton when I needed him?

Over the course of the next few weeks, I would come to understand that American boys "take a piss," they don't "have a piss," as their English cousins do. I have become a reliable source of entertainment: "Oh, Teddy wants to have a piss! Yuk, yuk, yuk."

While my parents are on a scouting mission, checking out other parts of these United States, I am staying with a cousin. I have been tasked with the daily mission of stopping at our new apartment to pick up the mail. My classmates are briefly confused, then amused, as I explain that "I need to stop at the flat to fetch the post."

Am I a target for a certain degree of mockery? Well, yes. But I have only recently emerged from three years in an English boarding school. British third, fourth, and fifth formers could offer their New York counterparts an advanced degree in hazing. Also, I had been a good soccer player in England. In New York of the mid-1950s, I am selected for All-City and All-State. That smoothed off some of the rough edges.

Adjusting to a new culture for a young teenager who already speaks most of the language is not that much of a challenge.

And I was, and remain, white.

Which brings me to my friend, Illah Nourbakhsh. (Even as I type the names, my laptop's spellcheck rebels, underlining both in red; as though to say: "You may want to check these names out again. They seem somewhat un-American.") Illah's experiences with being an immigrant are, in almost all respects, distinctly different from mine. Back in the day when I still had an English accent, it was considered, at worst, amusing, at best, rather exotic.

Illah's American English is not merely fluent, it is that of a highly educated and cultured man. But there's the hint of a slightly exotic accent, as though to confirm the darkest suspicions raised by that curious name.

Illah and I, each highly successful in his own field, each a thoroughly acclimated American in most respects, (I, for example, fall short in that I find baseball to be an excruciatingly boring game) have always and will continue to experience radically different levels of acceptance.

One additional piece of evidence from my side of the ledger: It is February 8th, 1961. My twenty-first birthday. It will be another two years before my beloved Grace Anne Catherine Dorney becomes my wife. For the moment, we are simply graduate students at Stanford: Grace Anne in a doctoral program, and I working toward a master's degree. We have just finished an extravagant birthday dinner we could ill afford. We probably had some wine. I am driving my '57 Chevy convertible in the wrong direction up a one-way street in San Francisco. A police squad car awaits at the next intersection.

"Oh, shit!"

The police officer politely requests my driver's license. He takes it to the squad car where, I assume, he checks my record. When he returns, he politely suggests that I turn my car around at the intersection so that we're headed in the right direction; and then, as he returns my license, he gives a slight smile and says: "Happy birthday."

Illah's experiences under similar circumstances tend to be somewhat different.

Read on.

Ted Koppel

Preface

Placerville, California used to be called "Hangtown." I remember this every time I am there, and I am there every time I stop for gas on the way to Tahoe from San Francisco. One winter morning, I pulled into the Placerville gas station around 5 a.m.—it was pitch black and serene, even though a blizzard was already raging in the Sierra Nevada range. I was heading into that blizzard, cross country skis in tow, to ski Elephant's Back, a beautiful back-country trail south of the lake.

Like most owners of 1980s Saabs, I regularly drove, foolishly, into dangerous snow conditions with my front-wheel-drive car, pretending that the old Swedish car had as much traction as a 4x4. It didn't. On my way out of the gas station, after turning onto the main road, I turned on my headlights, traveled an eighth of a mile, and parked to the side as a police cruiser, lights spinning, immediately pulled me over. Out the window went my license and registration, with plenty of "sirs" peppering my answers to his questions.

"Do you know why I pulled you over?"

"Maybe because I turned my headlights on after I was on the road, sir? I forgot to turn them on when I turned the car on. I'm sorry, sir."

"Where are you from?"

"San Francisco."

"No. Where are you really from?"

"I'm in college here. I am from Kansas City, Missourah." (I always drawled the last vowel for policemen so they could tell I wasn't lying)

"No. Where are you really from?"

Typical immigrant story. And it's not exactly about being born in another country. So long as you have olive skin, or a strange name, or the hint of an accent, this is what the cops always ask you. Even if you were born in L.A. (which we Iranians really do call Tehrangeles).

"Where are you from?" Actually, everyone asks the wrong question. They should be asking, "*Where do you belong?*" This is the question I hope to answer in this book; and the answer is unsatisfying.

My birth country, Iran, has been in conflict with my home country, the U.S., for nearly my entire life. That sets me up as an outsider everywhere. Transplant me to Teheran tomorrow and there is no way I can blend in and be accepted. My brother took a trip there and a taxi driver immediately asked him, "So you're from the U.S.?" "How did you know?" my brother countered. "From the way you walk."

Or take me to the customs and immigration zone at any U.S. airport and watch me have a Bad Day that makes me Interesting at Parties. I have witnessed fifty years of not quite belonging; and the small cuts from not belonging have shaped who I am.

Being from an exotic conflict country can be a superpower, at times. I can read your fortune in Turkish coffee grounds, and this has been an incredibly effective first-date move. I can combine spices smuggled in from Iran (via the Family Network) with yellow split peas from my Syrian grocer and French Fries from McDonald's to make a gourmet Persian meal that you will adore. I can impress modern-day American pagans with my over-the-top Spring Equinox Nowruz celebration, essential to every Iranian's heritage; and I can also wow every mindfulness and intermittent fasting guru when I fast for Ramadan all month long.

This book is about fifty years of navigating the space between cultures in conflict and how an immigrant can endure years of adversity, become resilient and successful, and still fail to arrive at a satisfying answer to the question, "Where do I belong?"

Introduction

I come from the Nourbakhsh ancestors who settled in Burujerd, a small village in the mountains of Iran. You will know you are in Burujerd when you see a giant teapot in the center of a traffic circle—a teapot that is itself a working teahouse. My ancestors were migrants, with even earlier roots in the Arabian Peninsula, and this likely explains a mixture of races that made some of my family members unnaturally pale-skinned. My mother's side brings in Turkish and Azerbaijani heritage—and Russian even earlier than that. This influence probably explains why people in Moscow and in eastern European cities will take one look at me and speak in their native languages.

This particular Nourbakhsh line also claims early participation in the mystic ways of the Dervish, an expression of Islam that turns away from material possessions and embraces the interface between Earth and Heaven. You have seen pictures of the Dervish whirl—right hand skyward, left hand downward. Spinning releases the soul from all the minute concerns that constantly invade our brains, creating a flow that divests the body from its normal connections and painting a space in which the heart and body can both become lost in a spiritual connection up and down.

I am not Dervish, although I would love to know more than I do about that way of life that is essential and plain, but also packaged and commoditized by traveling troupes on show for Westerners. But seeing and reading about that whirl, I find a strong connection to the interface I see the Dervish occupy.

For an Iranian-born immigrant in the United States, like me, everyone assigns categories like "bicultural" and "Iranian-American." But I don't buy into the intention of these phrases. Being bicultural suggests I am firmly in a category—that I have a tribe of those like me, just as a monocultural person might. These phrases recenter my identity in a comfortable space, and what they fail to recognize is that what people like me feel is not centered in our own special space.

I am not in one place or space or tribe. Rather, I am *in between*. Always in between, always watching the spectacle of conflict from an in-between space. That brings me back to the Dervish. One hand up, one hand down. In neither Heaven nor Earth, but dancing between them, acting like a conduit that exists in a third space.

This book is a personal exploration of the "in between." What about my development put me here, and how do I make sense of my particular dance along the interface?

The chapters that follow are vignettes from the age of six to the present day. I do not present these experiences chronologically; rather they are grouped in conceptually related families. Every story is entirely true, to the very best of my memories.

Chapter 1

At the Tone

click click click click click click click click click click click click click click click click click click **At the tone, twelve hours, fourteen minutes, coordinated universal time. Beeeeeep.** *click click click click click click click click click click click click click click click click click*

=================

I grew up obsessed with time. The obsession started when my parents purchased a Panasonic RF-2800 shortwave radio from Montgomery Ward. This was a gorgeous, black analog radio receiver with dozens of knobs and switches—every one of which served an extremely precise and narrow function, making the owner's manual a geek's dream. In movies, I adored any scene where a giant electronic board contained dozens of dials, switches, and knobs. The shortwave radio transformed this dream from fiction to reality, and I felt like a pilot controlling this machine. I had a poster of an early-model Boeing 747 cockpit in my bedroom, and I would spend hours staring at all the controls, clueless about what they all do. With the shortwave radio, I had my own cockpit, and I was able to discern and use every instrument in my home cockpit.

The shortwave radio sat on a glass slab, atop a carved, Iranian table. The artist had etched rose petals, a nationally beloved symbol, into the edging of the tabletop. The result was gorgeous, but impractical, since it was not flat at all. But the glass sheet took care of that, and a very modern, black, plastic radio finished the look.

The radio came with a reference book that listed times and frequencies for radio broadcasts from around the world. I quickly learned what Greenwich Mean Time meant, and how to convert from Kansas City, Missouri to GMT. I filled my evenings with journeys to distant lands, all on the radio. It was my public library for escaping the Midwest and dreaming about the great beyond.

When I encountered the frequencies for the national time broadcast from Colorado, I dialed into that set of frequencies and was hooked.

Dial this number now: (303) 499-7111. Take a listen for a solid minute and a half. Every second is marked. Every minute is announced. Once in a while, there is a double-click rather than a single-click, especially after important minute chimes, such as the top of the hour. I would listen at midnight, to hear "zero hours."

This was the time of cheap digital watches on the wrist, and I needed a watch that had a real second hand that would move with the radio's chime. So, off I went to the library, researching quartz watches with second hands that had the very best accuracy on the market. I saved up money and purchased my own analog watch—a Railroad Approved Seiko—because these were tested for second-hand accuracy, and they looked absolutely cool with twelve-hour and twenty-four-hour markings. Back then, the predecessor to Best Buy in North Kansas City was a local place called Dolgin's. I went there with my mother, with money in my pocket, and asked to buy this very special Seiko watch, which was expensive: one hundred dollars. The counter clerk took my mother aside and, within earshot of me, told her that she wouldn't sell me the watch. It was too fancy and fragile. I walked over, flushed, said I would take good care of it, and that was that.

I would pull the crown out, wait for the shortwave radio chime, push it in just at the right time, and then satisfy myself with the fact that, for days thereafter, my wrist's second hand moved in perfect synchrony with the national time broadcast's chime.

This was my version of control and personal agency, in a time of extreme lack of control, extreme uncertainty. The year was 1978, and eight-year-old me was witnessing the Iranian Revolution.

For my family, the story of the revolution was the story of life and death. My grandfather, a former governor and senator, had left Iran with nothing but his wife—and by the skin of his teeth. I suspect that if he had stayed two more months, he would have been one of the many four-star generals to be executed, when executions became a daily ritual in our home country.

Instead, he was with me, in Kansas City. He dressed up every morning: shirt, coat, and tie. He wore a traditional French beret and so I smile, to this day, every time I see an older gentleman wearing one. He had a small black notebook, and we took turns with the short-wave radio. He marked times and frequencies and, being a polyglot, he tuned in to frequencies from around the world, practicing his French, Russian, and English.

But the time of executions during the Revolution came, and my uncle, who led a major university in Teheran, was jailed as a political prisoner through an arrest process that itself could be a motion picture, so full of double-crossing and misdirection.

The new revolutionary radio broadcast from Iran was on shortwave, beamed to the whole world. It carried their grim news broadcast, and it always ended with the announcement of the names. The names of every political prisoner who had been executed that day.

I cannot give you a phone number for this one. But I can give you the feeling. My grandfather sits, beret on head and dressed up fancy, on the big chair in front of the carved Iranian table. I sit next to him, on a chair or sometimes cross-legged on the floor. We are in the foyer of the second floor of a suburban house in North Kansas City, wall-to-wall carpeting everywhere. And we listen to a list of names. He has his notebook open and sometimes jots down a name in Farsi. I listen to the names. Every name spoken that does not start with "Doctor" is a relief. A relief flushed immediately with guilt—because someone else's uncle just died.

Once in a while we hear "Doctor," and anxiety wells up inside me. I hold my breath and wait for the next word. My uncle's first name is Mehdi, and any name approaching the "M" sound was emotionally catastrophic.

We listened through all the names. Every day. For weeks and months. This was a ritual I did not accommodate to. Every day was a trial of emotion and fear, and every day I was afraid of tomorrow.

There were a couple of times in those weeks when the radio announcer said "Doctor Mehdi." That is when I would look away at the wall, focused only on the arrival of the next syllable.

The announcer never said my uncle's full name. Through a series of decisions and errors also fit for a Hollywood movie, he managed to get out of prison, get to the airport, and leave for the U.S. just as authorities discovered that they had released him in error.

More than three thousand political prisoners were executed by the revolutionary government of Iran. Listening to all those names, a dozen at a time, every day, transformed my relationship to the shortwave radio. I still wanted my watch to be on time—and, to this day, I am overly focused on having the time be right, to the second. But the shortwave radio stopped being an instrument for exploring the world and for exerting some personal agency. It became a loudspeaker for the grim reaper—one of many daily reminders, in those years, of just how little value lives might have; how little control I had over myself, over my surroundings, over my family. For me, the shortwave radio died with the revolution.

Chapter 2

Electricity Everywhere

We moved to the United States when I was young—but trips to Iran were a regular part of life, until the Revolution. I remember the final such trip well. It was 1976, and it was during Nowruz, our New Year's celebration that coincides with the first day of Spring—which to this day, I argue, is the very smartest way to begin a new year.

On that trip, we took the time to leave our capital, Teheran, and visit some of the most beautiful places in Iran. We traveled to Persepolis, and I still remember looking at the bas-relief images of half-horse, half-humans on the crumbling walls of Iran's ancient capital. My mother provided repeated commentary on the crimes committed by outsiders to Iran. Alexander the Great was extremely not-great for Iranians, having ransacked and burned our capital for the sake of a girl—at least in our telling of ancient history. We went also to Mashhad, to the most beautiful architectural marvels—mosques with millions of mirrored, beveled surfaces that reflect light in every possible direction. As Kipling wrote in *How the Rhinoceros Got His Skin*, "the rays of the sun were reflected in more than oriental splendor." That was pretty much a perfect way to describe the beauty of light in these houses of worship. I took turns sweeping the floor in these mosques—a great honor, because you submit yourself to the humbling act of cleaning.

Visiting shops, family homes—really, anywhere—there is one custom that always suffused every interaction and, to this day, makes me happy—and that is: life is tea, to reference the television show, *Ted Lasso*.

At every turn, you drink a delicious blend of Ceylon and Darjeeling tea, black, in a small crystal glass we call an *estekan*. There are sugar cubes, and nothing made me happier than putting the sugar cube between my lips, then drinking the hot tea through the sugar cube—a ritual I taught my friends in college years later. The tea had to have three perfect qualities: *labreez, labsuuz, labrang*. Filled to the absolute lip of the *estekan*; burning hot on the lips. And the color of lips: dark.

On this particular trip, for New Year's festivities, everyone offered me *qottab* pastries along with the tea—a half-moon filled with chopped almonds or walnuts with a powdered-sugar exterior sure to make a mess all over your clothes. I loved the combination—tea and sugar pastry—surrounded by adoring family, beautiful architecture, and delicious food.

Then there was an argument. A government leader was chatting with my uncle, my father, and others. The official boasted about the pace of development in Iran. "We have modernized the entire country. We have electricity everywhere now!" My family spoke up. "No, there are plenty of villages with zero services: no electricity, no sewage, no water." And so the debate was afoot. The official cited statistics and promised that things had changed—we were simply out of touch with the reality on the ground—his staff had informed him that electricity was everywhere now; end of story. And of course, my family, more stubborn than anyone ought to be when talking to powerful officials, resisted.

═══════════

So, the next morning, off we went. We bundled into cars—my parents and brother, my uncle and a few others—and we drove just one hour out of the Teheran metropolitan area. As you drive out of town, you witness a transformation that is literally a time machine. Westernized dress gives way to flowing *chador* outerwear—still years before the revolution—and cars give way to more and more bicycles, donkeys, and carts. Roads become rutted, and the landscape gradually turns from a park-festooned, lush cityscape to a desert with rolling hills, much like Arizona. We arrived, finally, at a collection of mud-brick buildings near a ditch.

In Farsi, this rural village is called a *deh*. It is an autonomous unit; it has some elders and some form of local authority; and it is a place rarely visited by the city folk who live with wealth, services, and luxuries. I had not been in a deh before, and I was not prepared for what I saw.

The dozen or so structures were one-room homes with dirt floors inside and out and mud-and-straw walls. Roofs were pulled together from whatever materials were available, with gaping holes in many walls—even numerous structures with no doors whatsoever, just a hanging piece of cloth across the doorway. There were no beds or chairs inside the structures—just cloth, blankets, and pillows. You sat on the floor. You slept on the floor. You cooked and ate on the floor. The ditch nearby was, in fact, the communal bathroom, and the smell took time to manage.

We walked from house to house. Children followed us. My father and uncle would stop at each house and talk to the inhabitants. They offered us tea with hospitality that made me feel like crying. They respected this visit by city people; and my father would take wads of cash out of his pocket and give each family a share.

I remember one home more clearly than all the rest. Inside it we met an older woman, who was yelling loudly and shaking. We visited her, and her yells continued. I never could make out what she was saying, but her family said she had been like this for years. My father was a doctor, and he spent more time with her, but to no avail. He gave them cash, too, and then after two hours, we walked back to our cars to drive to town.

I could hear the woman wailing, screaming, as we walked away. That feeling—of walking away from such upset as the sound gradually fades away—is with me today. I could hear her as we drove away. The very idea of electricity, in that moment, felt like a completely ridiculous concept, something from another planet.

This would be the first time in my life that I started to grasp the insanity of the concept: "We have electricity *everywhere*."

Chapter 3

Cassette Bee

M y father was a general surgeon, and that job demands that you create dictations of your cases—history physicals, office exams, operations. Dictaphone was the company of choice for dictation technology; they made a Microcassette recorder that physicians could carry in their pocket, whip out, and record away. The cassette itself was truly tiny—even in my small nine-year-old hands. His Dictaphone, which I was rarely allowed to use, helped me understand cassette tapes and was the first stepping stone on my path to music recording and playback. My regular cassette recorder was a cheap unit from Montgomery Ward that had C batteries and a power plug.

My cassettes were a pile of old Continuing Medical Education tapes that my father had grown tired of collecting. The tapes were the colors of hospitals and medical clinics in the 1970s: vomit green, mustard yellow. I would pop "Emergency Cholecystectomy" into the machine and give it a listen. It was, after about thirty seconds, completely unlistenable. The voices were droning, and nothing about the content could tug at me. The next step was total erasure. I would scour the house for some Scotch tape, then cover the broken-off tabs that rendered all educational cassettes read-only. Pay attention to this—because I was *really* good at erasing content after the tabs had been broken off. Broken off precisely so you wouldn't accidentally erase the contents.

Then I would tune a tiny radio to the local classical station in Kansas City, and I would put the little radio speaker by a microphone built into the tape cassette recorder. As soon as the music started, I would hit record and listen breathlessly, recording entire symphonic movements before deciding whether they were worth keeping or overwriting once again.

I was in charge of road trip music for the family, so I took these recording sessions very seriously, organizing tapes by style so that I could proudly play them in our Pontiac Bonneville as we drove for two days to reach the foothills of the Rocky Mountains.

I should explain that mountains are a serious national pastime for Iranians. Our capital city, Teheran, is ringed by the Alborz mountain range, so the weekends consist of picnicking anywhere steep, driving on impossible mountain dirt roads on underpowered stick shift cars (like VW Beetles), and then parking the car, spreading a blanket, and enjoying the cool mountain air with fruit and bread. There are, literally, Persian carpet cafes in Iran spread across giant boulders in mountain streams, where travelers stop and drink hot tea and have a communal smoke. There are cloth-tented tea houses along the streams with views of the mountains, more tea and Persian baklavas, and Lavash bread with Bulgarian feta cheese, walnuts, fresh mint, and fresh basil.

So, when we were trapped in the Midwest, every possible opportunity to travel two days to real mountains—the Rockies in Colorado in our case—was a celebration. My favorite mix tapes for these trips were a set of Lorin Maazel-conducted concerts, taped in Vienna for New Year's parties. It consisted of a maximal dose of Strauss—all the Strauss composers—with waltzes, polkas, and related tunes that always climaxed with a slow, emotional version of "The Blue Danube" waltz. After a complete childhood of recording and playing this stuff, I overdosed so badly that, today, I doubt I can sit through a single piece of waltz music.

My tape-recording days blew up, and it all happened because of a three-way collision between my overblown grit, the Iranian Revolution, and a spelling bee. To begin with, I should explain that spelling bees are a truly evil torture system for vast numbers of young children. Standardized tests, we mostly agree, are terrible. They quantify intelligence, which is total nonsense. They suggest that one test matters a great deal—more nonsense. They rank and order our children. They fail to capture our human qualities. They demonstrably fail to have any correlation with success in college or life. But at least they're not public! You and your pencil go into a room, suffer for several hours, and leave without any public demonstration of your failure. So, there is at least a modicum of privacy that we can hang our hats on.

Not so with spelling bees. They inhabit every one of the worst qualities of an SAT test, and then they add the innovation of real-time, public performance in front of friends, and real-time, public failure for nearly every child in the room, save one. Awesome. Then there is the teacher pressure and parent pressure of actually participating in this communal torture.

The game starts back at school, when my language arts teacher stages a seemingly innocent spelling bee in the classroom. "It'll be fun," they say. "Don't worry about it. Don't prepare." As an avid reader, I do fine in this little game. Stand up, spell a few words, and laugh it off.

Then everything goes to hell. The school contacts the parents. The parents are informed that I have qualified for the city spelling bee. The school sends me home with a book containing ten thousand words that I need to be able to spell. And this is where Angela Duckworth, Grit, TED, and childhood self-actualization theories all collide. So the story goes, the lifelong-successful spelling bee champions are the ones who locked themselves in a room and hated every moment of it but forced themselves to learn the ten thousand words. Alone. They did what they hated well, and so they will succeed in life. I simplify, but only a little.

Then there are the kids forced into spelling bees by their parents—the kids who were grilled on the words incessantly by their parents at breakfast, all weekend, at dinner. The theorists state that they don't show personal grit, and even though they become spelling bee champions, they don't succeed nearly as thoroughly in life.

But then there are the 99.99 percent of the rest of us! However we studied, we did *not* become spelling champions. In fact, we failed out rather early and sat there and angrily noticed we knew a lot of the words used later. But we failed. And that's what you learn. *Fail once and you're out.* So, I don't qualify for Duckworth's theory, because I'm an example of the spelling bee non-champion—the one who lost on his fourth word.

But there is more to this story than public failure. You see, many of us spelling bee non-champions were tricked into being in the spelling bee, and so we had little choice but to figure out how to memorize ten thousand words.

My solution involved my Montgomery Ward cassette player. The theory was outstanding: put a tape in, prerecord it with the word challenges, then a pause, then speak the correct spelling, and repeat ad nauseum. Then play back the tape, pausing after each word, spelling it and checking the answer. As a bonus, I would get to use my favorite audio tech rather than a book of words.

Now this spelling bee was happening right as Iran was violently passing from post-Shah revolution by socialists, communists, and clerics to theocratic revolution that killed off all the socialists and communists. And my uncle was still in prison.

He had managed to pull a coup, my uncle. He had found a way of recording a message to my mother—his sister—on tape and had gotten the tape smuggled out of prison. The tape made its way to family in Teheran, and from there, *par avion*, to our home in North Kansas City.

A tape from my uncle, in prison. Easily the most valuable cassette tape in the home, by many orders of magnitude. The only other tapes at home were either waltz, polka, or Continuing Medical Education. So, really, no contest for second place.

I searched the house a bit and found a tape downstairs after my inspiration about how to make studying for the spelling bee a whole lot more fun. The tape was orange and had no label. Definitely another ugly hospital tape. You see, when you smuggle tapes out of prison, you don't write on them: "This is a smuggled prison tape. Do not erase." You write nothing on the cassette label.

I set off finding some Scotch tape and very effectively covering the broken tabs, thoughtfully broken off so no one would ever erase the tape. I recorded several dozen words on Side A, and then I set off for the living room, sitting on the sofa, playing my tape and pausing it, one word at a time.

There is a cognitive dissonance that your mother encounters sometimes. A good example is when she's dusting the living room, and you are sitting there listening to words in your own voice, and then after a word, she hears a few syllables of her brother's voice instead of her son's voice. That's the textbook definition of dissonance. And panic. And anger.

I had wiped out fully half of his lovingly detailed message to us; and for the rest of that season, I got to listen to a couple of my spelling words, followed by my uncle's voice as my mother played the fragments over and over again, gleaning as much as she could from the partial message that remained.

I used the horrible, ten-thousand-word booklet after that and still pretty much failed the spelling bee. I do not believe Duckworth had an analysis for my category, but I am pretty sure it's not called grit.

Chapter 4

This Land is My Land

This land is my land. This land is my land. Go back to your land. Get out of my land. From California to the New York Island. From the redwood forest to the Gulf Stream waters, this land was made for only me.

F ourth grade P.E. is the worst class. It is a special, in-civilization version of *Lord of the Flies*. By the time they are ten years old, children are old enough that, actually, they are in charge. The P.E. teachers are blithely unable to notice what is actually happening in the gym, in the locker room, in the showers—really, everywhere. And the children are just old enough to have solidly formed opinions, muscle with which to impress their opinions upon their prey, and a literally unbounded amount of meanness to employ.

Now add to the normal bullying chalice of fourth grade P.E. a new special sauce, and it really starts frothing: fifty-two American hostages held in your home country, Iran, for 444 days. With deep coverage on the news cycle in my adopted hometown every single morning and evening.

Day after day, the hostages were not released. And so, day after day, fourth grade P.E. was a laboratory for innovation—how can we show Illah how unwelcome he is, since he's Iranian and, therefore, partly to blame for this disaster?

Through their musical talents, a group of boys in my grade developed alternate words to Woody Guthrie's song—a double-irony of course—and used this new song on me, in full chorus, during any outdoor P.E. day activities: baseball, running, hurdles, high jump, flag football. The basic approach was to encircle me with half a dozen kids, then sing using a solid shouting voice.

In the locker room, after each and every P.E. day, we had to change back into school clothes. I was sufficiently scared of this singer-gang that I tried every possible trick to avoid the unavoidable: shower late, shower early, use the coach's shower room. But it never really helped. No matter what I did, there always came a time when I was standing there with just my underwear on. That is when the group helped educate me by giving me a hanging wedgie. That is when you lift someone up and hang them by their underwear on a hook.

The problem with a year and a half of this was that I never knew when it would happen and how bad it would be. The singing, the wedgies; all of it. I teach today on loitering munitions and drones; I quote from P.W. Singer's book, *Wired for War*, about the disempowerment felt by residents of Afghanistan when they hear a drone buzzing overhead for hours at a time, sure that doom is facing them but totally unsure when.

Theirs is a mortal danger; mine was just child's bullying. Knowing, though, that something horrible is coming every day, changes your understanding of stereotyping in a very deep-seated way. It makes you extremely allergic to judging others, to making gross generalizations, to singling anyone out.

I'd like to point out that singling someone out has lasting effects. The P.E. teachers themselves did a good job of demonstrating this to me at my private school. I was a very skinny kid, moreso than you are imagining just now, reading this. As in when I threw a basketball, I had trouble making it anywhere near the net or backboard from the free throw line. So, in indoor P.E., when we played basketball, the teachers had us line up and take turns throwing baskets from the line. When I'd throw the ball, it would make it about halfway to the backboard—a truly lame arc that, to them, suggested I was refusing to try hard.

Their solution was elegant. They would have all the other kids line up and watch, and they would give me as many throws as I needed to make a basket. With everyone watching, they told the whole class that no one would be dismissed until Illah made a basket. And so I got to stand there, failing time after time, trying to lob the ball far enough to at least have a lottery's chance at making a basket. When I left that grade, I avoided touching a basketball for about thirty years.

Stereotyping, singling out, classifying—these are things we witness all the time. For me, I had a very similar feeling of dread when adult-on-adult versions of these interactions, in passive-aggressive ways, came to pass those very same years with my parents.

My father's light skin and odd appearance made it impossible for any stranger to guess that we were Iranian; and yet he had a strange accent that he actually nurtured—it was part English (from studying in England, maybe) and part Dr. Zhivago (from studying the movie, I suspect). I would be standing with him somewhere—anywhere. Ponderosa. Pizza Hut. Sambo's. And someone would ask him, "Where are you from?"

His answer was always, always the same: "Guess!" And there would start an incredibly uncomfortable journey with a bad beginning, a bad middle, and a horrible ending. Whoever it was—they just wanted a simple answer. Instead, they were lured into a guessing game. "France?" "No! Go further east." With some people, my father was trying to show them their geographical unsophistication. "Russia?" "No, go south!" With some people, there were no hints, just a "no, guess again" to show them their United Nations ignorance since they ran out of country names before guessing Iran.

Sometimes, eventually, there would be a weird, hard left turn when my father would say "Persia!" and the interrogator would suddenly be stuck, because they would know about Persian cats and Persian carpets, but what country is that? Sometimes he'd say "Iran" near the end, when every useful thread had been run. I hated, hated, standing there. I felt like I was part of a vitrine display.

The ending was always. "Oh no!" or "I'm so sorry!" Awesome. Pity the sinner, hate the sin? There was no nice way to end this mess of an interaction, and no amount of my pleading would ever stop him from playing out this gameshow.

You can feel this form of dread in all manner of other adult interactions that a child is forced to witness. Another of my favorites was the "Where's Mecca" gameshow. We would go to someone's house—likely a member of our mosque congregation, or an Iranian elderly couple who may or may not pray. My father would want to demonstrate his religious *bona fides*, so come prayer time, he would say that it's time to pray, which way is Mecca from their house?

They would point, what, southeast—because on a flat map, Saudi Arabia is toward the southeast. And the game would begin. My father would lecture on great circle routes, ask someone to produce a globe—and often one of their children would bring one to the living room. Then, using a piece of tooth floss, my father would demonstrate to them that actually, the shortest path to Mecca—as the Boeing flies—is northeast. Either the homeowner would politely accept this, feebly fight back, or become crestfallen at the thought that they'd prayed in the wrong direction since immigrating.

It's all power negotiations, and the knot I felt inside was the exact same whether the country-guessing-game was carried forth before me, or little children were shouting at me, "This land is my land!"

The bullying did end at school—and it ended before the hostage crisis ended. I finally got the courage, one afternoon, to hit back. I was basically naked, and they came over to give me the hanging wedgie. I launched out with a left hook that was laughably poor, but it made contact with one child's nose, and he started bleeding.

The next stop was a formal visit to the principal the next day, for me. I explained what had been happening—and throwing a fist was deemed far more punishable than singing a song with wedgies. So, I was sent home with a mini suspension.

What does this all do to a little kid? I cannot generalize, but I can tell you what it did to me, personally. We had an unfinished basement at home. All concrete floors, no fragile furniture. We also had old office chairs from my father's medical clinic down there, with spinning caster wheels all around the base. I would sit down there, in those chairs, and shove off the walls, from side to side, just gliding across the concrete floor.

When the shitstorm of bullying was in full fledge, it was a little different. I would go downstairs, turn off the lights, sit in a roller chair, and close my eyes. I would pray hard to God to let me cease to exist. End my existence so that I could just not *be* anymore. It would be such a relief.

Chapter 5

You're One of Us

It is so easy to learn that we do not belong, that we are not welcome. Divisions are an instant architectural marvel—easy to put up, like walls, and slow to remove. Otherness, stereotyping, caricaturing—all these facilities are the grout that hold walls in place, and children and adults alike habituate into their nonstop use.

So, how do we find belonging? In my experience, I have always found that the most generous and inclusive around me are those who are marginalized. They give the most of what they have, and they invite me in with authenticity. As I navigated middle and high school, I found belonging in three groups of compatriots: Black high schoolers, my goth friends, and the Jehovah's Witnesses. My relationship with each group was distinct, and yet it was the diversity of these three groups that, together, fed my sense of togetherness.

By the time I entered high school, my private school boasted a student lounge, where we could hang out between classes. But it was not remotely cool, and so most students entirely avoided the glass-walled bubble of a lounge. So, I found myself in the lounge, repeatedly, with the tiny number of Black students who managed to be at this private school in the heart of Kansas City, a town with a significant Black population that mostly could not afford this high-end, expensive education. It was in this space that I remember a mantra repeated to me often—to a skinny, pale geek with spectacles who studied, and studied only: "You're one of us."

Those words convinced me that there was an "us"—that my relationship with the world was not one of just *Illah v. The Universe*. Those words, repeated often, also set up a synchronicity—a recognition that hurt or loneliness or victimization can itself start to define the togetherness we can share across culture and skin tone.

With the goths, my exploration of belonging took a turn into daily, after-school debate practice. When students say debate, they often mean team debate, which is a decades-old practice of speaking impossibly fast and scoring points through the use of epic piles of notecards that present volumes of fact—quantity over rhetorical quality by a vast margin.

As I was entering high school, a new format was up and coming: Lincoln-Douglas debate. This format slowed down the speaking style and presented a stage for one-on-one debate where rhetorical power and value-oriented discussion was featured—argument and emotion rather than speed. I fell in love with L-D debate, and joined the high school debate team thanks to a charismatic history teacher and after-school debate coach.

My daily compatriots in L-D debate practice consisted of a handful of goths. They were sarcastic, smart, funny, bookish, and highly anti-establishment. They dressed the part—all black clothes, long overcoats in hot Kansas City weather—and they had "Say No to Nancy" buttons on their bookbags and coats; signs of the times.

I spent an hour every afternoon in the library with my debate team. The goths had the self-confidence that I lacked. They read every news article with a cynical eye, wondering who the author was, and what their truest intentions were. They naturally resisted the instructions of every authority figure and talked openly about the shortcomings of those in positions of power throughout our world, local to global.

Here was my high-speed seminar series in critical inquiry and in negotiations of power in society—all from a roomful of fifteen-year-olds. They thickened my skin daily and tempered my sense of materialism. They showed me how to sit, how to chill, and dip into long, authentic conversations about politics, drugs, injustice.

Today, my children can sign up for electives in high school such as Power and Protest; but in my Kansas City world of the 1980s, these peers were my teachers, planting the seeds of justice-seeking that would stay with me and crystallize into my career aspirations.

They also welcomed me. I was obviously different—a Muslim Iranian kid in polo shirts, playing soccer and tennis, and befriending teachers— some of the very authority figures they resisted. Yet they always welcomed me into their circle, and never suggested that I become *like* them, even in a subtle way. Instead, they simply accepted me as the token *other* in their circle.

With Jehovah's Witnesses, my connection is complex: barbecue, some Montessori, and surgical risk.

The first thing you always hear when you walk into Gates & Sons Bar-B-Que is a loud, fast "Hi, may I help you?" There are competing barbecue franchises in Kansas City, and every resident has an absolute belief in the supremacy of one of them. But Gates is the only one with this greeting, and it is a much-loved reminder that you are home, at Gates. I grew up deeply convinced that this was the best beef brisket in the world and, honestly, nothing in my half-century of living has convinced me otherwise. I spent hours enjoying the food, tilting back in my chair, and looking at the network of ceiling fans, all driven by a single, impossibly long belt drive.

So, you can imagine my excitement when my mother's Montessori pre-K classroom welcomed children who were the direct descendants of the Gates owners. My mother's classroom was an astounding space of religious diversity on the ground floor of a Catholic school—Notre Dame de Sion, run by the Sisters of Notre Dame. They had hired my mother, a Muslim, and welcomed her as directress of the entire Montessori program. When Catholic Mass occurred in the Chapel, all students who did not participate would congregate in my mother's huge classroom, where she would welcome their differences. Here I witnessed a form of acceptance that was the very ironic opposite of what I witnessed in my own non-parochial, private school across town.

The Gates relatives were generous and loving toward my mother and toward me—I often helped set up the classroom for each season of

Montessori-oriented discovery, from changing leaves and plants to the math station beads and, of course, servicing and cleaning the giant fish tank. I remember birthday parties with delicious beef brisket from Gates laid out for all—with us invited too—as well as holiday cards and check-ins well after their children had graduated.

Some of these relatives had one other distinction, which wove its way into a narrative of risk-taking and belief absolutes that I grappled with at the time: they were Jehovah's Witnesses. This part of the story involves my father, who was extremal in the full sense of the term. He believed in moral certitude: there was right and there was wrong, and everything could fit entirely into one or the other category. Belief had to be absolute; confidence in belief equally certain. Yet, as is often the case with those who value totally binary paintings of the world, my father would intellectually respect others with absolute beliefs, even if they contradicted his own tenets.

And so it was that I witnessed the ways my father, a general surgeon, navigated a world where his views were, to say the least, impractical. General surgeons do basic abdominal work such as gall bladder removal, appendectomy, colon repair, and hernia repair. They depend upon family physicians to make referrals. But my father was part of no practice, and he was not interested in the parties and socialization that would endear him to Kansas City family doctors. So, he struggled through scant referrals for a lifetime. He believed that his work had inherent merit, with no need for marketing, for friendship, for trust-building and politicking.

But there was one place where his absolutism actually endeared him to an entire community, and that would be the Jehovah's Witnesses. Their faith forbids them from accepting blood transfusions—even their own blood after the fact—and even in the face of certain death from blood loss, say following trauma or unexpected blood loss during surgery. Surgeons face the brunt of this challenge, because a Jehovah's Witness is likely to refuse required surgery unless the surgeon promises not to conduct a blood transfusion, even if a major artery were accidentally ruptured during the operation.

I think the family physicians and the other surgeons in the city saw my father as a very odd specimen; but this they learned and held close: send the Jehovah's Witnesses to Dr. Nourbakhsh. My father would sit with the patient, enthusiastically explain to them that we all worship the one and same God, and promise exuberantly that he would avoid all blood transfusions during the surgery, even if it meant the death of the patient. This made my father a solution pathway for Jehovah's Witnesses in need of emergency appendectomies, cholecystectomies—everything abdominal that can be lifesaving.

I watched from the margins, in hospital and in my father's clinic, as Jehovah's Witnesses expressed their admiration for his willingness to operate on them, on *their* terms. They were kind to him, and he was absolute in his willingness to risk their lives in order to save their lives. There was a kind of ultimate mutual acceptance in the air between them—an acceptance that entirely transcended the fear of death, the fear of malpractice lawsuits, and the fear of regret.

Decades later, every few years, there is a knocking on my door during Thanksgiving dinner. I open the door, and there stand two well-dressed Jehovah's Witnesses, gospel in hand and ready to recite their opening statement. I ask them, right away, if they're Jehovah's Witnesses, and when they nod, I launch into the story of my father and my childhood, explaining to them how, long ago and far away, their congregation admired and welcomed my father, because my father made a pledge that few surgeons could endure.

I tell them that we are Muslim, and I welcome them into my home for a chat. Their mission, knocking on doors, is usually entirely forgotten. They ask questions about my father, about Kansas City, and relax. I tell them, "You are one of us."

Chapter 6

Flow

What makes me happy? And what makes me happy but does not get old, year after year? Psychologists use the term "flow" to denote activities that are all-consuming, occupying the mind and body so fully that anxieties and obligations are crowded out entirely. I stumbled into my versions of flow with two teachers and two activities: sailing and pottery.

My first memory of sailing comes from the most cramped quarters of my life. I was skinny and short in middle school, and my future chemistry teacher was, at the time, the carpool driver who took me to school daily. He was an outstanding woodworker, and he was busy making a beautiful, wooden racing sailboat, an E Scow. The E Scow is twenty-eight feet long and feels like the Ferrari of sailboats. It is narrow, long, and totally lacking a heavy keel. Instead, it has symmetric twin centerboards protruding at angles, so there is nothing keeping this boat from flipping over except the sailor's skill.

When my teacher was putting a railing along the bow of the boat, he needed someone to hold the nuts under the deck while he tightened the screws from above. I was happy to take the job on and still remember the smell of wood varnish; the very hot 60-watt light bulb in a metal jacket that occupied the tiny crawl space with me; the wrench in my hand; his voice coming through the deck, muffled; and the nearly unbearable heat.

I began sailing with him on the weekends, learning how to manage the jib then to handle the tiller, balancing the mainsail's angle, the wind, and the heavily leaning boat as it hummed across the tops of the waves at Smithville Lake, north of Kansas City.

Those summer days were perfect. The lake was ringed by trees, and the sounds of wind jostling leaves mixed with the splashing of the bow. As the boat sped up, under absolutely ideal conditions, its entire hull would resonate, humming loudly. The boat sang, and I could hear the singing through the tiller—a kind of giant musical instrument.

My eyes would dart between four near emergencies constantly. Where is the coastline? We have to tack before running aground. Where are all the slow boats on the lake? We have to thread a path between them all. Is the sail luffing? We need to change direction or trim the sail. What do the red threads on the mast and the sails say about the wind direction? We need to make the tiny corrections that make the sailboat fly through the air like an airplane wing on its side.

This sort of boat is not about relaxing and reading a novel. You are making corrections *constantly*. Not a second goes by that you aren't changing direction, adjusting your seating position, leaning out more because you've tilted over forty-five degrees while smiling giddily. You are controlling a machine right on the edge of controllability; the wrong puff of wind can flatten the sail and turn the boat over.

My ultimate compliment—the one I strived for on every tack—was when my teacher would leave the jib's sheet cleated as we flew down the lake. The moment he thought we might be out of control, he would pop the sheet out of the cleat—it makes a loud snap—and I would know I'm on probation. Years later, I would realize I do the exact same thing teaching my children to drive using an old, stick-shift Mini Cooper—if I put my hand on the parking brake and prepare to yank, they're on probation.

Sailing this way is a whole-body experience. But it is more. It is about actively operating on an edge. There is risk and disaster around the corner, and I am navigating with my muscles and my brain, with all my senses tuned in, to avoid the disaster with never-ending corrections that force me to stay entirely in tune with the *system*—the lake, the wind, the ship, my mentor on the jib.

When we pull the boat back up on the trailer and put it in the boat yard, I am mentally and physically exhausted and thrilled. The anxieties I faced earlier seem more surmountable, more contextualized. It is hard to overstate how much the experience contributes to self-confidence, mental calmness, and a personal sense of poise.

Pottery found its way to the same place in my heart; and it was the unlikeliest of pathways. When I was in third grade, in private school, we had an art class in which we used markers to draw patterns on clear 35-millimeter slides that we then put in a slide projector with a round carousel. I adored the combination of light, projection, and color, and I was engrossed in creating thick boundaries of color by pushing the markers, hard, onto the slides to make abstract, bleeding images.

The teacher came over, stood by me, and said, "You are bad at art." Well. That was it. I stopped, and I mean I stopped, for six years. I repeated the mantra, "I am bad at art," for years, and refused to do more than the absolute minimum in any art class thereafter. It is hard, in retrospect, to imagine that a single teacher's flippant comment can have such a thorough impact on a child's self-identity. But it is so very true.

What happened in high school finally shattered my caricature of myself, and it was through a teacher's patience and accommodation. Our art department head managed all the arts, but the bulk of his space was dedicated to clay: several kilns, an outdoor homemade Raku kiln, clay-making equipment, dozens of glaze buckets, several electric pottery wheels, and one old-fashioned kick wheel with a John Deere tractor seat.

In class at first, we began experimenting with three-dimensional form—sculpture—and I was hooked on the structural challenges of expressing myself with a material as malleable as clay. When we earned short bursts of time on a pottery wheel, I was stunned by the level of difficulty. More often than not, lumps of clay became round cylinders, then collapsed back to lumps as we overworked them.

My teacher's art studio had an open door, always, and I started spending hours every day there after debate, working to knead my clay to just the right consistency, and then practicing centering and lifting the clay on the wheel, sponge in hand. My teacher let me use the kick wheel, and that is where I found a duplicate weekday version of the flow that sailing gave me on weekends.

The kick wheel, for me, is perfect. A heavy platform, at the lower end, is suspended on high-quality bearings, resulting in silky smooth rotation that is much slower, and much more even, than anything an electric wheel can offer. The wheel itself is dead quiet, and so the sound enveloping me is that of the sponge and my fingers on water and clay—slapping, sliding. I am forever bent over the clay, right hand along the clay's exterior boundary, left hand inside the clay body, feeling the wall of the vessel as I pull it up. Every moment demands corrective forces, but all movements must be gradual; work too quickly and everything goes to ruin.

I operate the wheel right along the boundary of failure. If I spin the wheel too quickly, the clay will accelerate outward and fail. If I wet the clay too much or move too slowly the cylinder will melt down, collapsing into a lump. If I try too hard to achieve perfection, the artwork will stop improving and will backtrack—over and over again this lesson hammers its way into my brain.

Pottery teaches me to move constantly, but slowly. To respect the substance in front of me, and to always consider if I am going too far—trying too hard to perfect what never needs perfection.

Working with such fragility crowds all else out of the mind for hours at a time. When it's over, I am soaping my hands, then trying to re-moisturize my hands because all their oils have been sapped away. There is a sense of elation that pervades me. The joy is identical to the feeling when I am pushing grease into the bearings of the sailboat's trailer, happy to be preparing the contraption for its next trip to the lakeside launch ramp.

I still have a kick wheel and try to find time to throw, but the demands of fatherhood and adult life make daily art impossible for me. There is also a bittersweet baggage of memories that clouds such work with every year that passes.

A decade ago, I spent several months making each member of my CREATE Lab some pottery, customized to each individual member of our research lab. I drew strength from that expression of care, and yet when COVID struck, we lost much of our funding, and furloughs ensued. Ironically, I was in the midst of making a new set of pottery gifts for CREATErs; but suddenly, half of them were leaving the lab, for good.

Today, the pottery wheel also reminds me of this reality of life; that no matter how hard I try to create a space where researchers can innovate for social good, their careers are still at risk at any moment that we fail to find another year of funding. Our work is transient, but shards of pottery last thousands of years in the dirt. My teacher used to say that regularly, and it took time for me to really understand.

My third story of flow is about piloting small aircraft. But that immediately raises a major barrier: aircraft are expensive! So, we need to back up and talk about college, money, and jobs. When I entered college, I thought I would be concentrating exclusively on conventional studies. I was bookish. But within six months of leaving home and beginning the journey of really, truly maturing, I recognized that, for family financial reasons, I needed to find a way to make money—real money to cover all my costs in order to become independent.

My solution was to work on the side. But I discovered that a side job cannot quite cover all my costs; so I worked three jobs, simultaneously, while trying not to fail out of Stanford. Back before the internet, finding a job meant hunting for adverts in newspapers and message boards on campus. The ad that caught my eye said, "Be a Kelly Girl!"

My first job turned out to be for Hewlett Packard, just through the Kelly temp services agency as the contracting organization. HP was flying high in the late eighties, so I said yes instantly. I was assigned to a visually impaired young programmer who was working on implementations of TCP/IP for HP. Transport Control Protocol is one of the most essential layers of communication software that enables our computers to interact with one-another on the internet, and my job turned out to be just perfect.

I was armed with a small tape recorder, boxes of binders on a weekly basis, and a straightforward goal: enable my programmer to be able to review all the information in the boxes by turning the documents into spoken word. Some documents were manuals on TCP/IP and related protocols. Some were software architecture writeups. Many were published papers from conferences, complete with flowcharts and graphics.

The job was intellectually satisfying on so many levels: I got to witness internet innovation in its infancy, and I also learned to take the written material and compactly describe it, from tables and charts to sidebars, into the fastest-speaking, clearest diction that my mouth could handle. The perspective shift from visual media to spoken word was fulfilling and different.

My programmer, Vera, was kind and sharp—an outstanding role model for me as I imagined a possible career in technology. At times, our conversations turned poetic. When I had to transcribe color-coded images, we would talk about the feel of the colors and develop our own shorthand for how to represent color in ways that could preserve the original author's intentions but knock us out of visual metaphors entirely.

My HP/Kelly Girl experience lasted years, through my undergraduate career, and it also exposed me to the HP corporate world. I walked the halls of HP, read the postings on the walls, and saw how programmers teamed up, met in meeting rooms, and occupied tiny cubicles in vast, open-plan high bays. The idea of Silicon Valley was a romantic, exciting notion to a freshman; the reality of walking its corridors made it seem, to me, approachable. This gave me both the courage to imagine being part of Silicon Valley after graduation and the power to walk away from it.

There was, however, not enough money in one job to satisfy the costs of college. And so, I sought out the on-campus, part-time work that many students find. I would take a class, enjoy the subject, and then ask the teacher if they had any side work for a student. My first success came out of a mathematics class taught by a German professor who was patient and reflective, to the degree that I started to understand math with a depth that had never before touched me. I asked, and he answered; and I lucked into another revolution in-the-making: The Genome Project.

The Genome Project was in full tilt, aiming to sequence the human genome and then learn how to read this codebook—how to crack the language of DNA and amino acid sequences to understand our identity, bottom-up. The math laboratory I joined was dedicated to Computational Molecular Biology: how to use the power of computer analysis to make sense of the sequences that were quickly arriving at our doorstep thanks to new, massive efforts at sequencing human DNA, animal DNA, and viruses.

I was in the midst of introductory programming and computer science classes across campus, so I had learned all the newest tricks for how to organize information, search it rapidly, and encode these complex calculations in ways that would run quickly on modern machines. In the math lab, we needed to quickly find recurring patterns in DNA sequences and amino acid sequences; and we needed to create software packages that biologists could use without deep knowledge of computer science. At the same time, we wanted to answer an almost infinite number of "why" questions—and one of these questions became our work's additional focus.

Our question revolved around the behavior of a class of proteins called Leucine Zippers. These proteins' amino acid sequences have the amino acid, leucine, in every seventh position. For some reason, some of these proteins zip together, literally, as they coil together. Some proteins do it with a copy of themselves, some only with others. Still other proteins refuse to zip together at all.

The Human Genome work was life-changing for me in numerous ways. First of all, I test drove the life of a researcher, complete with a big computer in a tiny, windowless office. I was inexperienced and naïve, but I was going to an office, doing research, co-writing articles, and even visiting a college that wouldn't let me in two years earlier, Caltech, for a conference on computational biology.

I was also witnessing how techniques in computer science do not live in a vacuum. I could take a new computer programming technique, implement it for an authentic biological question, and concentrate, not on the tool as having inherent value, but on its application to deep human questions.

The way we introduce technology to young students, it is extremely tempting to fall in love with the technology as an end in and of itself. Over the years, I have had many arguments with computer scientists that see true invention, within computer science, as the greatest good they can perform. But when, early in your career, you begin applying technology to human problems—facing Human Papilloma Virus daily on your computer screen—your attitude about the hammer in your hand evolves, and this in turn can have downstream consequences on your thoughts regarding electives, career choices, and a lifetime's impact on society. In essence, the Human Genome Project helped me fall out of love with technology, and that has served me well.

During one conference speech, my colleagues and I presented our work on using machine learning to understand how Leucine zippers work and what shape they take. We were at the top of our game, using biological metaphors and terminology that we had steeped in for about a year. The head of the Math Department lab stopped us after the talk and told us that we sounded like real biologists. He was not one to provide faint praise, and this was the most positive comment I had ever encountered from him. It filled me with a sense of the possibilities—that I could be someone, someday, in the research world.

There was one other life-changing effect from the Genome Project that is worthy of mention, stemming from the fact that every colleague I was working with was much older and more experienced than me. One afternoon, my closest colleague announced that he was taking me out to dinner in San Francisco. We shot off in his car, and he explained to me that we were about to eat raw fish for the whole evening.

Growing up, I had encountered sushi in just one way. When we would head to the big downtown Crown Center mall in Kansas City, we would walk by a restaurant with big windows in front. My father would point and tell me that people there were eating raw fish. *Raw. Fish.* I would stare in through the window, and he would tell me to stop staring. This happened every time we went to Crown Center for a decade; and here I was in a tiny Japanese car (Honda) heading to San Francisco to partake.

The restaurant was in the Outer Sunset; I remember this because, years later, I was eating there with friends and was in total shock when I realized Robin Williams was sitting directly behind me. This first night of my life in a sushi restaurant, some thirty-plus years ago, I experienced wave after wave of new flavors and textures. And I loved every one of them. The joy of discovery that came from such total novelty is a feeling I will never forget. To this day, my children and I love to go get sushi. But not a minute goes by, when I eat sushi, that I do not remember the feeling of that first evening.

So, two jobs, one on campus, one off campus at HP, were paying the bills, mostly. But I took a class in Logic in the Computer Science Department, fell in love with the subject, and wondered if I could add a third job to my little collection. It turned out, the professor agreed to mentor me, believe in me, shepherd me into graduate school, help me obtain a Ph.D., and guide my intellectual development more than anyone else at university.

The timing, once again, was remarkable because this professor's research lab, The Logic Group, concentrated on a systematic and formal approach to understanding how computers could make decisions and plan using their imperfect knowledge of the world. I was welcomed into the community of Artificial Intelligence, just as this topic was enjoying a new revival.

Years earlier in the 1970s, AI researchers had begun promising AI to the world. Thinking that Artificial Intelligence would bootstrap, perhaps like a five-year old, researchers reasoned that once they have basic problem-solving and learning working, then their artificial progeny would learn their way to ever-greater capabilities bottom-up. And so, the AI revolution seemed just around the corner, perhaps years away, but certainly not decades.

Money poured in, often from the U.S. Department of Defense, for researchers to build intelligent systems that reach that magical inflection point; and then the research community discovered, over the course of years, that what they promised was far harder than they had anticipated. Building from the ground up would require a solid foundation, and a theory for how, with some sort of cruise control, the system could self-improve from there forward.

But the foundation was problematic. The digital, static logic of a computer needed to capture the uncertainty and nuance of an organic, ever-changing real world, and this language was hard to codify, in terms of time, dynamism, and uncertainty. And even with a foundation, researchers needed to invent authentic learning, where a computer could improve its performance over time.

While this was possible for limited cases, like playing checkers, it was entirely unclear how to make learning something that could be applied to more than a single case at a time. Researchers could not even agree on whether a piece of software really implemented human-like learning, or whether it was a mathematical trick that performed well under conditions so constrained that it did not reveal any deep insight regarding true thinking.

By the time I was an undergraduate, researchers had retrenched, then pushed forward with significant progress in all manner of Artificial Intelligence grand challenges: common sense reasoning; reasoning about time; decision-making while uncertain; reasoning about data in databases. All these topics were enjoying a new spring thaw, and so my new job at the Computer Science Department handed me a front-row seat to the second major blossoming of AI at Stanford, one of the institutions at the heart of the effort.

My advisor challenged me with a simple question that would take years of exploration: When should an intelligent robot stop planning and start acting? This question is an offshoot of an age-old issue called "bounded rationality." In regular parlance, military spokespersons often talk about known unknowns and unknown unknowns. As humans, we have this special ability to acknowledge that our own ability to understand a situation is limited; that we can only make decisions with a limited amount of information and a limited amount of understanding about the true implications of our actions.

We are meta-cognitive, able to have a conversation, not only about what to do, but additionally about what information we are missing and what knowledge we need to gain in order to, later, be able to discern what to do. Bounded rationality is our frame of mind when we are not too conceited as to think we have all the right answers. Yet it remained an open challenge to design a computer system that understands its own limitations, and then reasons around them.

We started with simple toy examples of on-screen robots exploring a maze with unknown goodies scattered throughout. The robot's job was originally to get to a goal position without being eaten. And yes, in 1993 we switched, once I became a graduate student, from a robot in a maze to a dinosaur in the jungle. *Jurassic Park* had been released, and dinosaurs were far cooler than robots.

My challenge was thinking up when the robots should stop planning their path through the maze, or jungle; and when they should start exploring, to gain more information and make progress toward the goal—even if their informational understanding of the world was imperfect.

My days consisted of charting possible thought processes by pencil on giant sheets of paper at the dorm; bicycling furiously with new ideas to the Computer Science department; and unrolling these giant sketches for my professor, excitedly discussing whether any of the tricks we were inventing were worthy of publication. Where the Genome Project was all about convivial research in a large team of biologists and programmers, my artificial intelligence work was all about personal innovation, in turn reflected by one very patient mentor—my professor and supervisor.

In the Genome Project, we vied to make new, useful tools for the community. In artificial intelligence, we attempted to invent completely new recipes for decision-making—techniques that were as of yet undiscovered. And all the while, my Hewlett Packard Kelly Girl work eschewed personal invention altogether, focusing me on close readings of basic texts about the underpinnings of communications technologies that would, in just three years, become the building blocks of the World Wide Web.

Two ruptures interrupted this three-ring circus just as I was hitting my stride. First, the math professor discovered through a financial reporting form that I was getting paid to do research in the Computer Science department. He asked me to his office and expressed his strong disappointment toward my disloyalty. Students were never supposed to work two jobs at the same time, and this violation upended any trust he had in me. After two years, my time in the Genome Project was over.

At the same time, I was finishing my junior year and was already panicked about locking in a job upon graduation. My solution was to chase the dream that was, to me, the one and only obvious choice: Bell Labs. I had grown up in the age of Bell Labs, when so many inventions had blossomed out of that place that it developed a legendary position in the eyes of us geeks. People said the hallways had white boards along all the walls, so researchers could stop and share ideas *anywhere, anytime*.

It was said that once you were at Bell Labs, you were there until retirement, at the forefront of technology innovation in the U.S. The only brand I remember as fondly in that age is NASA—that is how highly regarded Bell Labs was in those times.

So, I interviewed at Bell Labs for a summer internship and, after two rounds of anxious interviews on the telephone, I got the offer of my dreams: a summer at the Disney World of Technology. The rupture was not this dream offer, which I was convinced would lead me to a lifetime career at Bell Labs, but my AI professor's response when I gave him my news.

"No. Stay here. I can pay you to do research at the university all summer. And then you enter our Ph.D. program and get your doctoral degree."

To put you, dear reader, in my shoes, I need to explain something. I had never thought of or talked about the idea of graduate school. I honestly did not even know what graduate school meant. My version of the world— which is often the case with immigrants as well as great numbers of students from non-academic family backgrounds—was that you get a college degree, find a job, and work that job until you retire. Even at a premiere institute, Stanford University, and with exposure to all these research experiences, I had failed to grasp the possibility that college can lead to more college, and after that it can even lead to a university job.

I stayed that summer, and I continued to do research. My advisor co-authored a publication and I began to understand the academic pursuit of scholarship, innovation, and writing. Before long, I applied to graduate school. Unlike all my peers, I applied only to my existing school, figuring that if I were rejected, I would return to the plan I had all along of heading into a career.

But I was accepted and continued into the Master's and Doctoral programs with my very-same advisor and mentor. The fragility of this pathway—the ease with which I could have gone to Bell Labs instead and been there when they essentially started shutting the place down three years later, is remarkable. A single, strong piece of advice really can be life changing.

This takes us finally back to flow. Working three jobs enabled me to pay the bills, but it also provided me with more than enough money to pay the bills, and therefore I was, for the first time, able to imagine becoming a pilot. All my childhood, I had built, flown, crashed, and rebuilt remote-controlled aircraft with noisy gasoline engines. I definitely spent more time building and repairing them than flying them; and I daresay the joy I derived from working on them with my hands gave me stability and therapy throughout my teenage years. I had spent hours on the first version of Microsoft Flight Simulator, landing and taking off at Meigs Field in Chicago and flying over Manhattan and the World Trade Center towers.

So, when my bank account made it possible to realize the dream, I was off to Palo Alto Airport, only ten minutes from campus, to begin introductory flying lessons. I loved sailing and pottery, but the university gave me no access to sailboats—just windsurfers—and no access to pottery beyond a depressing electric wheel in a chain link-fenced basement studio. So, I threw myself fully into flying.

To the outsider, flying seems like driving, with the addition of height and a whole lot of risk. But to a pilot, flying is absolutely nothing like driving. Driving requires medium concentration, and is a tool, albeit a really entertaining one, to get from place to place. Flying a tiny air-plane is never about the destination. And the process of being a pilot—of inhabiting that space even recreationally—is only partly about manipulat-ing the airplane's controls as you fly.

Where driving relegates you to the artificial space of the human-built roadway system, flying frees you to fend for yourself in the wilds of nature itself: among billowy clouds and above cities, coastlines, mountain ranges. Flying is like hiking Cloud's Rest at Yosemite and seeing the world from a grand place, as opposed to walking a sidewalk from the Target parking lot to the storefront. Different planets, truly.

And the preparation required to do that flying in the wild is to driving like snow camping in Tuolumne Meadows in the dead of winter is to taking a stroll in town. You prepare, and you anticipate, and then you fall into a world in which you are bit player.

The background preparation for earning that pilot's license, and using it, is a dream-come-true for anyone who wishes to cross multiple disci-plinary boundaries. Piloting demands intimate knowledge of mechanical and electrical engineering. You have to know exactly how every part of an airplane works so that if anything ever goes wrong in flight, your model of the airplane's inner workings enables you to rapidly find a workaround that keeps you alive.

Flying requires intimate knowledge of weather patterns, from the theory of air currents and moisture to reading real-time weather maps, predicting future patterns, and reading the clouds as you fly between them. Federal Aviation Regulations governing flight consume hundreds of written pages, so you learn to attend to every detail of the regulations and make considered decisions about altitudes and directions of flight, experience requirements to fly passengers, airspace restrictions, and hundreds of other topics.

Radio work between the pilot and ground control is its own, unique lan-guage. You learn a new cadence, lingo, and process for respecting lines of priority and supervision and yet working the system to obtain the clearances you need. Flying demands constant emergency procedures practice, taking any high-strung individual, like me, and retraining my nerves to calm down and patiently diagnose emergencies without any room to panic and flail.

Finally, piloting is the ultimate multi-tasking practice. You look for traffic, physically navigate, reference a map, check up on weather, communicate with air traffic control, and check the airplane's sensors for health—all at the very same time.

There is no room in this swirl of activity for worrying about anything else—you simply have to perform, and you learn to make corrections constantly, never settling but trying to improve on every dimension. This is ultimate flow and, just as with sailing a small racing scow or shaping a wet and fragile cylinder of clay, you are navigating the edge of success and failure with great care, nonstop. For me, this is the perfect adventure.

There is though, in flying, one other gift that has no equal. The airplane and helicopter, from three thousand feet up in the sky, deliver us a view of the world that balms the soul with perspective. The foothills to the Pacific Ocean become wrinkles on a vast scale. Car traffic becomes red blood cells on an arterial system. Clouds from above are unspeakably beautiful, and they pull your vision to the horizon. The ocean coastline is endlessly stimulating—it literally never, ever gets old. This perspective shift is perhaps the greatest gift of flight because you land at the end of an hour exhausted from the juggling flow of flying and elated from the perspective shift of being so far above. That combination creates an afterglow that lasts days and provides a renewed energy and patience that I always find essential.

My undergraduate experience was a complete juggle. Flying provided perspective and flow. Three jobs taught me about the internet, AI, and the customs of university research. I fell in love with the culture of the university, and I became ready to commit to it entirely. It would become my home culture for the ensuing thirty years.

And yet when I look back on the undergraduate experience, the least important part of all was the coursework. I matured, developed, loved, and committed to inquiry and invention—all in side projects, side jobs, and extracurricular obsessions. The curriculum was useful; but the life-changing events of my college experience were never, ever in the classroom.

This recognition would echo resoundingly, years later, when pundits and even professors I knew announced that the traditional university was going extinct thanks to Massively Open Online Curriculum—MOOCs. This was to spell the end of the era of the university because we were going to democratize university learning to every bedroom around the globe.

The original message, and the venture-fueled, audacious visionary statements, were complete nonsense to me. Yet another example of how a perfectly decent idea, warped by the feedback cycles of venture capital and magical thinking, can be sold as the revolution that it isn't.

To this day, I wonder—the professors who were so convinced of MOOCs upending conventional universities—did they have experiences like mine in college? Did they really just take a massive load of courses, ace them all, and overachieve their way to academic posts? Or do they just refuse to acknowledge the deeply social nature of their own personal experiences struggling and navigating their comings of age?

Chapter 7

Will You Marry Her?

When I was a sophomore in college, a stranger in Tennessee proposed to me. To crush the suspense: I didn't marry her. But the anxiety, at the time, was extreme—I remember the deer-in-headlights position of being caught with a decision looming over me: stay or run?

This all started with the unfulfilled promise of electric cars. Contrary to what half the population says even today, we knew in the 1980s that the climate was on its way to hell and that we needed to move away from fossil fuel consumption. Among my engineer friends, we talked nonstop about electric cars and how California's Air Resource Board, CARB, would be instituting rules prescribing how many electric vehicles each major car manufacturer would have to start selling—at the latest—by the year 2000. The deadline kept slipping, and CARB would get sued by the major car companies, all to stop these rules from forcing innovation. The manufacturers said that electric cars were totally impractical, and therefore CARB's rulemaking was costly and also impossible.

But a counter-narrative was strong in our circles—General Motors had created a beautiful, teardrop-shaped electric car that could charge as it drove, thanks to solar panels covering its upper surfaces. GM's Sunraycer won the World Solar Challenge in 1987, traversing Australia, a land with well-paved roads and loads of sunlight. So, we were all staring into the future and then seeing political business machinations push the future we wanted further and further away, toward an unknowable date.

In the midst of this mixture of hope and frustration, GM established a national solar car challenge, promising to send the top performers to Australia. Called the GM Sunrayce USA, this would be a race amongst United States university teams, who would build solar-powered, electric cars from scratch and then race them from Orlando to Detroit.

The poster on campus drew me in—and hard. Within a month I found myself, as a freshman, on the Stanford SUnSUrfer team along with some twenty diehard gearhead-environmentalists with one Quonset hut, two faculty advisors, and zero funding to our name.

The challenge was a steep one for novices: design, fund, and build a brand new solar-electric race car that could participate daily in a one-thousand-mile, all-weather race, then get the car, a logistics team, and a group of drivers to Florida.

As with all projects, the first step was food—and we struck gold. Not only did we manage to convince PowerBar to provide us with literally a truckload of energy bars as our sponsor, but we also won over Gatorade with a corporate sponsorship, giving us literally infinite quantities of Gatorade with which to wash down the energy bars.

Concerned for nutritional balance, I ventured to Hobee's, a Palo Alto brunch institution that bakes probably the best coffee cake on the west coast. They agreed to donate us their leftover coffee cake every day—all I had to do was drive there once daily and take possession right out of the kitchen. This, for the next year and half, was our principal diet, seven days a week. You will be unsurprised to learn that, for the rest of my life, I will be unable to smell, let alone eat or drink, either Gatorade or PowerBars. We computed at one point that we had each ingested at least one hundred pounds of each—enough to change our body chemistry forever.

Donations were part of my job, and the car's body parts were largely built from the seconds of corporate donors. Ciba-Geigy gifted us honeycomb composite-based sheeting normally used as flooring in Boeing 747s—material that is strong and lightweight, yet can be sawn and re-attached with epoxy, just like plywood. The skeletal structure of the SUnSUrfer was made with these boards and notched and glued just like a balsa wood model airplane kit, or a piece of IKEA furniture.

A local window company, Southwall Technologies, provided us with a giant acrylic sheet and hours of time in their walk-in oven, trying to pull the acrylic over a form to create the doubly-curved windshield. Although this attempt eventually failed, the nights spent at Southwall were memory-making. Wait outside the oven while it gets impossibly hot. Have eight of us walk the acrylic, heavy gloves on our hands, into the oven. That's right, walk right into a very hot oven. Hold your breath so you don't burn your lungs. Pull the acrylic over the form as hard as possible, then run out of the oven before burning to death. Then repeat over and over, trying to get the curves just right.

The process of "gluing" and assembling the car's structure was even more time-intensive: make giant vats of epoxy resin. Pull donated carbon fiber woven sheeting through the resin, then do wet layup by hand-applying the carbon fiber to all the joints and forms. This process was literally never-ending, running for days.

There is a limit point—after a certain amount of zero sleep and heavy resin fumes, combined with Gatorade and PowerBars, all of us would start giggling uncontrollably. It was a sort of late-onset mania that, we felt, was not quite impeding the work itself. So, we carried on. There was one particular time when we were awake, nonstop, for forty-eight hours doing wet layup. I had my ancient Saab 900 hatchback there at the Quonset hut, and we just had to finish the resin before calling "time."

The interesting part is that I next woke up in my own dorm room, wondering how I covered the three miles from the solar car site to the dormitory. I still remember that morning, wandering campus in search of an old Saab—which I did find, about halfway between work and home.

The mentors that helped us throughout this year-and-a-half project saved us. They included a mechanical engineering professor and a brilliant working engineer who had invented everything from micromachines that he used to make surgical microsurgery tools to thirty-foot-high bicycles for Burning Man. Even Phil Wood, quite possibly the best wheelsmith on earth, agreed to create custom-spoke wheels for our race car. To this day, I use Phil Wood's tenacious grease on my bicycles, because every time I look at the green container and his signature, I think of this gentleman who was so generous to a group of truly clueless teenagers.

General Motors eventually loaned every qualifying team a brand-new Chevrolet Lumina van; and so, our Lumina, our truck carrying the racecar, and an old Volkswagen Vanagon all set out for Orlando, listening (no, really) to The Wall, on repeat, for the entire drive through Texas.

The Lumina actually saved us because the car was so funny that it kept us awake through every monotony imaginable. We discovered very quickly that this van was the most unreliable car any of us ever had the pleasure of driving; and we further discovered that the entire interior of the car was assembled without the use of screws or glue. It really was snap-together. So we—and in fact, many teams at the time—resorted to calling the van a "Lemona"; and we proceeded to lead the field in discovering how much of a Lemona can be disassembled *while you drive it to Florida.*

By the time we arrived in Orlando, the interior of the car was unrecognizable—the dashboard was essentially nonexistent, as were all interior ceiling and door trim pieces. In our hurry to impress all the competitors with our little project, we forgot that someone, eventually, would tell GM about the experiment. So, the bigwigs from General Motors came to our camp and gave us threats about how, if we did not reassemble the car by morning, our parents would all be buying this vehicle.

The race itself, from Orlando to Detroit, was thrilling. It was a life-changing experience along multiple dimensions. I was one of three drivers; and the experience of sitting on the recumbent bicycle-seat and controlling this machine on a country highway was magical. The car was totally silent, except when you pulled a special lever to slow down by charging the battery, it shrieked.

The controls looked as if a bunch of children had made a make-believe car—knobs and switches everywhere—just what gearheads dream of when they're six. Except, in this case, every knob and switch actually did something. There was a two-way radio for keeping in touch with the lead and trail vehicles (cellphones did not exist yet, dear reader). And as driver you were glued to your amp-hour-meter, trying very hard to cover the distance as quickly as possible without using too much energy. This meant coasting the downhill sections, creeping uphill at best efficiency. We slowed down in bright sunshine to let the batteries charge, sped up under clouds and rain to get to the next bright patch. And we never, ever, touched the brakes—every use of brakes was energy thrown into the waste bin during an electric race.

Driving was exciting, but logistics was an equal joy. I would wake up early to look at the weather outside (the internet did not exist either). I would find a pay phone and call the FAA, posing as a pilot looking for the area forecast. We used that forecast to establish a strategy based on cloud cover along the path, and then planned when to stop and charge, when to race fast, when to crawl carefully.

I remember stopping on a country highway in Tennessee to charge the car along the side of the road. A farmhouse was just next to us, set back with a large yard. Out came the gregarious family, and in we went for homemade lemonade and sweet tea as the racecar charged, its entire back section tilted up for the best solar angle. The generosity we repeatedly felt along country roads warmed me—I came from a place and time where generosity from strangers was never a given, and this gave me an optimism for rural America that, today, never extinguishes.

In Indianapolis, we got to race our cars around the Speedway, and I happened to be driving during that section of the race. That was my first and last time on the Speedway, and I remember the tilt of the road, the feel of the pavement, distinctly. In Spring Hill, Tennessee, GM arranged for us to tour the one and only Saturn factory. Saturn was a whole new style of car company—no haggling, generous benefits for factory workers. We talked to the workers and toured their state-of-the-art exercise and shower facilities. They were happy and proud of this new American experiment in fair labor and transparent marketing. It did not end well; but at the time, it felt like a demonstration of the future awaiting us all.

In Bowling Green, Kentucky, GM took us to the Corvette factory. Just imagine—a bunch of gearheads who have built their own car, getting to go *inside* the one and only Corvette factory, seeing the cars in every state of assembly. The most memorable scene was a hands-on examination of the suspension system. This massively powerful monster car had suspension hardware that was impossibly thin. To save weight and make this supercar the fastest it could be, talented engineers had managed to make its metal parts the lightest and thinnest they could be while withstanding the shocks of racecar driving. That elegance was, aesthetically, the most beautiful thing.

Each evening, we would camp with all the other competitors in the Sunrayce, and this was a study in contrasts. Some teams were wealthy beyond measure. University of Michigan had funding and engineering from GM—they were a feeder school to GM's college hiring program. Their car, their team, and their equipment operated at a level of sophistication that made our team and our entry laughable.

Some teams were friendly, and we enjoyed chatting in the evenings, but no team matched the friendliness and generosity of the Puerto Rican student team. They had traveled the furthest, and they had scant resources; but they were always my favorites to hang out and eat with or just to relax with after the tenseness of the day.

On the last night that all the teams had together, the Puerto Rican team gave us each a tiny carving on a leather band. I still have that carving today, hanging on the top of the guitar stand that carries my favorite guitar. Every time I walk over to pick up that guitar, I recall that team's kindness, and the elation of a shared adventure.

There were moments of true adversity. Once, when I was driving the car at a fast clip, the single rear tire blew out. The car began fishtailing badly, and I didn't touch the brake pedal because it only actuates the two front wheels; I was afraid of a spinout and total crash. Instead, I started pulling on the regen lever, slowing down the rear rim to weathervane the car straight. It worked, and I pulled over. But the threat of totaling our much-loved machine had my heart pounding.

Another time, I pulled out of the starting gate with the logistics team driving behind me, and I followed the printed map instructions for the

racecourse. But they made a wrong turn in front of me. Every previous day, as we drove through waving crowds in small-town America,
there was a Vanagon and a Lumina sandwiching me. But in this case, I
ended up on Main Street, the lone solar electric race car, just humming
along with zero surrounding vehicles. The children were waving and
smiling, and this made any nervousness about my predicament evaporate. I waved back, drove through town, and felt like a small rock star.

That same morning, I pulled into a factory parking lot because there
was no support team and I needed to know the weather conditions
up ahead. So, imagine this: I parked at a textile mill in Tennessee.
I opened the space age cockpit cover and stepped out. My uniform
consisted of gloves and a full-face motorcycle helmet with an attached
two-way radio. So me, my gloves, and my full-face helmet all made
our way into the front reception area of the mill. There, I took off the
helmet, explaining to an older woman that I needed to please borrow
a telephone to call the FAA for a weather forecast for my solar racecar
out there in the lot.

The mill was filled with workers—and many were young ladies,
about my age, all of whom got up and went out front to take a look
at the car. The manager showed me to a telephone, and I got to work
dialing the FAA and requesting my forecast.

When I was all done, I took my map, notes, gloves, and helmet and
made for the front office—from the phone in the mill high bay. When
I thanked the manager, she asked to have a word. We sat down, and
she explained that one of the young ladies working in the mill really
liked me. A lot. And was wondering, would I marry her? I remember
the moment, because the manager was not smiling or laughing. She
was entirely serious, and very interested in my response.

I remember my answer in the haze of a teenager caught utterly off
guard. I mumbled about the race, about how I had hundreds of miles
to go, and that I was still studying at school. My heart was pounding;
and all the rest of the day, all I could do was wonder, ridiculously, if I
had just made the biggest mistake of my life.

The final race stage arrived, and we met our families at the finish line. The SUnSUrfer finished roughly in the middle of the pack of cars that actually made it the whole way, and for that we were both proud and disappointed. But this is where the project took a turn that gave me some insight into my own motivations and my sense of responsibility. We had a celebratory meeting with all of us engineers on the team, plus some of our family members. At this get-together in Detroit, the heads of the team spoke excitedly about the next step—how we were going to learn from this car and build a much-improved machine, from scratch, to race in the next GM Sunrayce in two years.

I listened silently to the enthusiasm behind this venture, then spoke up, saying that we had talked all year about how our true goal was electric vehicles for everyone on city roads, to do what it takes to convince drivers that they ought to be driving electric cars, and to convince companies to convert to electric. I said that building another car would be just about entering another contest; it's time to take our message to the people and the government, to advocate for the change we must have, even as CARB is kneecapped by industry.

The debate that day in that conference room was brief. There was overwhelming interest in building another car for another race—this was the spirit of the room. I was the outsider for thinking that building another car was not productive. I became angry and silent and walked away from the team and their efforts, which did indeed mature into several more outstanding solar-powered race cars over the years.

I was, in a word, impatient. I saw my time in college and beyond as very finite—a short fuse that needed to be planted in a truly productive direction. I desperately wanted to build a practical, electric car for commuters; studies for years had noted that people only travel twenty miles to and from work on average; this was easy even with conventional battery technology in the eighties.

My dream was to fundamentally change society. Engineering, to me, had to take a back seat to social change; and engineering that is not explicitly pointed at positive social change—I had no appetite for that kind of innovation, even though it could be groundbreaking and tantalizing.

In the university, to this day, I am often surrounded by those who derive enormous personal satisfaction from the ingenuity of a new invention. They are truly happy when they have discovered the unknown hidden under the surface of all that is known. But my heart cannot operate that way. I am entirely unhappy until I have made a change, however prosaic, that I view as a tangible improvement to someone's lived experience.

When I make a coffee mug someone will enjoy; or teach a class that students love; or make an air quality sensor that a community uses to increase fines on a local corporation—that is when I feel useful. The SUnSUrfer project was my first glimpse into my interior motivation by showing me the alternative narrative that drives me.

Chapter 8

They Ride Camels

A merican war was not at the forefront of my worries when I entered college. We had seen present-day war as I grew up, but with little participation by the United States. The Afghan War was an early memory for me—a reminder during the Cold War of the Soviet Union's designs for expansion. This war prompted repeated stories by my grandparents of the Anglo-Soviet invasion of Iran in 1941, as they could distinctly remember packing and leaving the north, in a panic.

Of course, the Iran-Iraq war was always in our conversations as I grew up, with more than half a million dead among two countries that share countless customs and religious traditions. The image of the two countries' soldiers stopping the fighting at noon so both sides can pray, then resuming killing each-other, were stories we told for years, trying to make sense of death on a massive scale.

The Falkland Islands war was jarring, because it demonstrated a super-power (at the time, Britain felt like a superpower) taking on a much weaker Argentina; it echoed the Afghan war, but the strident nature of the over-whelming force that Britain brought to bear demonstrated a kind of war power that, at the time, felt new and scary to me as a twelve-year-old.

I entered university after a period of relative calm in terms of U.S. warf-ighting, and even relative calm globally. My distance from geopolitics began to collapse in the spring of freshman year, when we saw news of protesters gathering at Tiananmen Square. I called my grandmother—a refugee in Boston from the Iranian Revolution—to excitedly talk about democracy in China, and she batted away all my optimism. "They will be killed tomorrow. Everyone knows it." She said this as if she had received a secret military report from on high and was absolutely sure of the outcome. I fought back, suggesting that the numbers were too great for violence to quash progress.

Then I woke up the next morning to news reports of the Tiananmen Massacre. *Tomorrow.* She was exactly right. I remember standing on a concrete porch at the end of the Paloma dormitory floor, looking out at the trees and pavement of the university. I was imagining a vast square filled with people, and then the violence, the blood spilled. There is an optimism about the world that you can nurture and grow, with each day that springs no bad news. But when the real world collides with your hopefulness, it invites in a cynicism and an anger that does not fade quickly. That is where I found myself—pessimistic and anxious in a universe where this level of violence could really occur at any time.

It was the next fall, as I started my junior year in college, that the very rough ride began. I was working all three jobs, and my first evidence regarding the scale of the first Gulf War came in the form of my AI professor, coming in late, talking about how hard it was to stop looking at the CNN footage of bombs falling in Kuwait and Iraq. I got hooked on the news, and I read and watched every piece of coverage available as the United States led a coalition of countries pushing Iraq back out of Kuwait.

I listened carefully to the language of the media's coverage and the Department of Defense's press releases. Technology was rife in the stories: smart bombs were proudly announced to be 98 percent accurate, with minimal investigation by the press. Then came stories of extreme suffering as apartment buildings and schools were leveled, followed by exculpatory proclamations about arms stored in those schools, followed sometimes by weak corrections months later that, actually, the school was just a school after all. The same press coverage would print the 98 percent accuracy stat at the top of page one, and then months later correct that number to, say, 30 percent in small print buried in the back of the paper.

I became hypersensitive to two things: technological infatuation and bigotry; and so I began collecting stories of both. I had a small, beautiful, lacquered box the size of two closed fists. The box was from Iran, and it was made of tiny bits of wood all glued together in geometric patterns, with a top lid covered by a hand painted scene from Ferdowsi's epic poem, *Shahname*. A photographic detail of the box top serves as the cover art for this book.

The craftwork of the box is what we call *khatam-kari* and is one of the beautiful handmade craft exports of Iran. I vested my anger, my sense of injustice, and my hatred of stereotyping into my khatam-kari box. Each article that suggested the infallibility of our smart-bomb technology—I cut out the key paragraphs with scissors, folded it carefully, and put it in the box. Every later story backtracking on the success rates—noting that smart bombs are not so safe for civilians after all—those went in too.

Press at top establishments vied with one-another to interview U.S. military jet pilots, and they published choice quotes from the pilots' perspectives. I read about pilots telling the press that when they dropped their bombs, they saw people on the ground "scurrying like mice." I cut that out. "Scurrying like mice." It enraged me to see that level of dehumanization told, recorded, printed, repeated. There were dozens of quotes, but one stuck with me because I heard the exact same words again, in rural Texas, on a road trip. This first time, it was a pilot, talking about how easy it was to fly in, take out targets, and shoot down Iraqi fighter jets. He said, "How can they fly airplanes? They ride camels." I cut that out, and this quote lived on top of the pile of papers, in my khatam-kari box, for years.

My second brush with this exact language came during a trip to Oklahoma City for a robotics contest that I was to judge, in 2010. I had figured out that the easiest way to get from Pittsburgh to Oklahoma City was to fly commercially to Dallas, rent a car, then drive north. So, I traveled three hours north on lonely roads, with only the AM radio stations available in the rental car. That previous night, a Pakistani airliner had crashed, killing everyone on board—it was a horrific accident. And my three hours on the road involved listening to the early-morning talk radio shows across Texas. The hosts were laughing about the Pakistani disaster. Laughing. They kept saying, "How can they fly airplanes? They ride camels." And then they would laugh again.

In 2010, driving and listening to that, the sense came back to me that I felt, nonstop, during the First Gulf War—the realization that I simply do not belong. This is not my safe space. These are not my values.

As I was filling my news box, I began to do some research, following a report on the possibility of a general draft in the U.S. How likely would it be that I would be called up to fight? I learned enough to become seriously worried and began to share my concerns and findings with my closest friends. Their responses—to the one—shook me: total lack of interest.

"Illah, this is really depressing, I don't want to think about it."

"If it happens, it happens, don't worry twice."

"I have my classes to worry about; I cannot spend time worrying about a draft."

My teenage friends were uninterested in the war, uninterested in their potential role in it, uninterested in how their tax money financed future conflict. I stopped talking to them about the war, about a draft, about smart bombs—we studied, we worked, we played volleyball. That was the bubble of the university.

I did find the people I needed, and they were a dozen sixty- and seventy-year-olds at the Peninsula Peace and Justice Center, just two miles from campus in the heart of Palo Alto. These individuals had historical perspective—they had witnessed an America at war before—and they were sensitized to the stereotyping of the "other" that facilitates our willingness, as a nation, to sacrifice the lives of other nations in the name of a greater good. I protested, organized, and marched—almost entirely outside the university campus, in the much more action-oriented streets of the adjacent town. I welcomed events and heard indignant speakers talk of cultures of supremacy and superiority of civilian deaths uncounted, of press cheerleading and parroting Defense Department reports to the letter.

Together, we watched police officers and FBI agents take pictures of our gatherings, our cars' license plates, and put us on lists shrouded in mystery and, therefore, open to our wildest imaginings. Finding a place to air my grievances, to share in a sense of shame for the scale of casualty—this was critical to retaining my sense of balance during my junior year.

One personal, family story remains with me, because it gave me an insight that the press was simply not covering. My uncle worked at AT&T, and the Department of Defense contracted AT&T to install new telephone switching equipment in Kuwait and Iraq, since our bombs had destroyed that civilian infrastructure completely. So, my uncle flew to Kuwait, traveled throughout the country, and helped install massive, portable switching systems that would bring the countries' telephone systems back online. On his way into the zone of destruction, he described traveling along the road from Kuwait City back toward Iraq. The Iraqi soldiers—all conscripts who had no heart in the fight—had been retreating in a massive line of vehicles, from armored personnel carriers to tanks, back to the Iraqi border after their defeat was assured. My uncle said that the line of vehicles was unimaginable; it stretched for miles and was entirely, thoroughly carpet-bombed, with destroyed equipment and dead soldiers throughout.

He passed this carnage—carnage in retreat—and when, a few weeks later, his team traveled back to Kuwait City, there was not a single hint of this bombing run. The evidence had simply evaporated—it was a clean highway sided with desert sand. He was struck by the efficiency of the sight's removal; and he was also stunned by the scale of destruction, and death, that he could clearly see during a massive retreat.

He told me this story on his return, in person, and for me, an active anti-war protester by night and university student by day, it made sad sense. My universe was polarized strongly—and this is before the internet deepened our divisions. On one side, I saw total apathy about a war that demonstrated United States power, technical prowess, and courage. I saw the press, politicians, and the Department of Defense as members of the very same team, with neither critique nor accountability available at any step. On the other side, I saw a minority of individuals who saw deep injustice in the execution of a war—with misery and no real follow-up plan that would improve that part of the world after this demonstration of shock and awe.

My personal response to this polarization, and to the injustice surrounding us, was to chase a sense of catharsis through activism. This belief in action—and in a personal need to act, always—became a central aspect of my identity thanks to the First Gulf War. Even though my childhood saw a relative paucity of United States wars, the time ever since, following the birth of my children, has been the exact opposite. We have been a nation at war for more than 90 percent of my children's lives, and so the injustices of war that make my heart break have become the constant drumbeat of lived experience.

Chapter 9

My Little Drone

Illah's Futureproofing Formula Ingredients:

> *1 future (F) you really want*
> *1 judgement utterly out of your hands*
> *1 alternative future (AF) that is entirely doable*

Decide that F is probably out of reach, and therefore stop worrying about whether it will happen or not. Set up AF with care, and spend all your time on its details to crowd out thoughts of F. Once you are sure that AF is going to happen, engage in some magical thinking to decide that whatever judgement occurs no longer matters at all because AF is really as good as F. If the judgement goes in your favor, become pleasantly surprised, stop fooling yourself about AF, and embrace F after all.

In grade school, I was unfairly judged thanks to the hostage crisis, with daily sentencing that created the trauma of ritual pain. That trauma made me hypersensitive to any situation in which I am judged. So, I engineered a strategy to avoid the anxiety of judgement. That was why my pathway to graduate school forged a way to reduce my stress rather than maximizing my chances of obtaining a graduate degree. I was ready to launch a career at Bell Labs, offer in hand. My solitary grad school application was an exercise in spinning the roulette wheel, just to see if I could achieve what was, to me, barely even a dream. This scheme for tricking myself into avoiding the anxiety of judgement became the dominant strategy that I have used at every major career juncture in order to face judgements outside my control, from faculty hiring and fundraising all the way to the tenure decision.

In this very first application of my futureproofing technique, the fates and, more accurately, my undergraduate AI research advisor, gave me a golden ticket into academia—a world I barely understood and would come to love over the next four years. But not without drama in parallel. These four years would coincide with three major milestones that would refine my academic identity: the birth of the World Wide Web, my first test match on military funding of AI and robotics, and the beginning of the dot-com boom.

There are scores of books about the birth of the World Wide Web, but I think what is most underreported is the total anticlimax of the WWW's first few months. My first explorations began in the hallway of the Computer Science Department, where a handful of computer terminals connecting to Stanford's main computing infrastructure provided us with access to a brand-new idea: a web browser called Mosaic. For us in the early days, using Mosaic was an act of exploration; we would create web pages, and we would visit others' web pages to garner inspiration for what else to add to our own pages.

The content of the pages we bartered and shared were just lists— lists of other great pages, lists of our favorite things, from recipes to simple services on-line that were just becoming accessible, like a temperature gauge in San Francisco. It was as if the concept of a bookmark was nearly all there was to the World Wide Web—it was fundamentally helping us share favorites and do so on a national stage with people we did not know.

There was no way that bookmark-sharing could foreshadow what the internet would become today. The creature we see today did not simply evolve gradually from its infant form. It shape-shifted in the most radical sense possible.

One way to fully embrace the unbelievable disparity is to understand what we did *not* see with Mosaic, sitting on chairs in the hallway. No advertisements, no money, no fishing, no deception, no weaponized information, no political radicalization. Mosaic was simply a format for sharing simple ideas, at first; and it was a platform only available to a tiny, highly privileged segment of the campus.

Lifelong expectations can be influenced, downstream, by initial impressions; and for me, the infant World Wide Web created a totally inaccurate first impression. I remember, back in grade school, when cable television was unleashed, the vendors promised advertisement-free viewing. The entire value proposition was that customers pay a monthly fee for cable and no longer sit through ads every ten minutes while watching their favorite shows.

For me, of a particular generation, that is what cable television was meant to be; and so, today, if I turn on a television in a hotel room and go to the "cable" channels, I can only be deeply disappointed every time I see an ad, because a promise from forty years ago is constantly being broken.

The internet holds this same disappointment for me. In my college bubble, this tool was a simple sharing platform. Today's web browsers are a never-ending disappointment—as screen real estate disappears to adverts, and as the content itself hews far more strongly toward manipulation than information, the whole experiment feels like a very sad shadow of what could have been.

My close brush with a second major trend during my graduate school career came from the blossoming of artificial intelligence in the nineties, with strong engagement from the United States military in how this new level of machine intelligence could significantly disrupt how we fight wars and protect our nation.

AI researchers were selling hard and selling well, noting that increasing compute speed meant that machines, with the right intelligent algorithms, would soon be able to outperform human beings at decisions in the complex environments of logistics, battle decisions, surveillance and formation control—all crucial aspects of how the U.S. would maintain long-term military superiority.

Early in grad school, I was busy taking the AI research I had started as a senior and applying it to the control of a robot arm that, like a gantry, could pick up and move chips on a large breadboard. The idea that computer code could push on the real world—making a physical robot arm pick and place computer chips at lightning speed—was novel and exciting. Computers were mostly walled gardens that could only change their own memory banks; the idea of programming for physical ramifications in the real world was far more enticing to me than staying locked in the software realm.

I worked hard to make this laboratory-based gantry robot perform planning and chip manipulation, and still I had the aftertaste of the First Gulf War on my palate. Those days of an international war, the threat of a draft, and the protests I helped organize were never far from my thoughts.

These two worlds collided during a research group meeting, in the form of a last-minute request specifically directed at me. It turned out that my research was funded by the Department of Defense. And the DoD funders were coming to the lab for a visit and for demonstrations. Would I port my RobotWorld code to a battle tank simulator, to show how an autonomous, AI-powered tank could make automatic decisions about where to point its turret and when to fire at the enemy?

I sat that night, home alone, wondering what to do. The power structure in a university research lab is clear—the professors are in charge, and they know best, and they guide your work. And the doctoral students do what they are asked to do. I had thought long and hard about personal participation in war—such as through a general draft—and I had also studied, informally, how high-tech weaponry such as smart bombs were stupid, not smart, and how their very name justified an increasing use of bombings that, otherwise, may have been questionable because of civilian deaths.

But two things had never, ever occurred to me. First, that my research was being funded by the Department of Defense. Even as I struggled against war, my workplace could be running on funding that explicitly supported ever more advanced technologies for war. And second, that anyone at the DoD was seriously considering applying artificial intelligence—the pursuit of human-style reasoning in computers—to warfighting.

I had already gone through the legal work of registering with Selective Service as a conscientious objector—I had a letter in my little box of special documents from them, acknowledging my status, and I now faced the requirement to create an AI battle tank demo in a matter of weeks?

The next one-on-one meeting I had with my professor, I worked up the nerve to broach this subject with him. He knew I was from Iran; but he had no knowledge of my anti-war activities or my political persuasion. And so, I told him, and I remember shaking from a sort of shyness as I spoke, that I was literally anti-war, and I just could not see myself creating a tank simulation, nor could I imagine working on a DoD-funded project.

He did not miss a beat. He instantly said, "Fine, then, don't do it. Why don't I buy you a small mobile robot and you can switch and work on educational robotics?"

Just like that. With no pushback, he fronted an utterly different idea, and he cooked up a research direction that, in fact, became my research destiny for decades: educational robotics. I had never even heard of that field and, to be fair, I think he came up with the idea as he spoke it. But using robotics in educational settings to teach AI? Sign me up.

We purchased a robot from a local company, Nomadic Technologies, and what followed was a fusion of two of my joys: engineering and AI. These robots were a nascent product, and by taking one on, I was accepting the fact that it would break regularly, and Nomadic's engineers (who were also its owners) would guide and help me learn how to fix it: sonars, wheel motors, belt drives, power boards. I learned to repair it all.

At the same time, my professor purchased me a Macintosh PowerBook 140, and I fashioned a Lexan mount atop the robot, suitable for carrying around the robot's new Mac-brain, which I would program in the AI programming language, Lisp.

The excitement I derived from the gantry robot that moved chips around was totally defeated by this trash-can-sized mobile machine that could navigate the halls of the Computer Science department and, eventually, the entire outdoor quad at Stanford. I spent hundreds of hours outside programming the robot with my colleagues, pushing around a wheeled cart on which we had extension cords, drinks, and lunch. Every day, all day, in the California sunshine. Everyone stopped and asked about our little 'bot—this was 1992, well before mobile robots roaming around outside were anything but science fiction.

My core research on navigation with this robot took us far. We eventually named the robot Dervish, and it wandered its way to national contests and some notoriety. But the educational side of our collaboration also took off during graduate school. My professor taught a class on AI, logic, and reasoning. He added a laboratory course that students could sign up to take, concurrent with the lecture course, that we named Mobile Robot Programming Lab (MRPL). We acquired four identical robots from Nomadic and designed a student group challenge that spanned the entire quarter, from low-level motion control of the robot to communication and collaboration between a team of two robots as they collected scattered "gold" pellets from the walls of a giant cardboard maze.

MRPL was a life-changer for me. My advisor gave me the reigns to teach this class, and I fell in love with curriculum design, lecturing, and designing and staging massive student contests. The class attracted students who cared about the whole stack—hardware, engineering, and AI software. Teams invented fantastical solutions, in the best cases creating robots we called Vaders—able to smoothly spin through mazes without ever stopping and turning. Think of a stunt car driver parking a Mini Cooper without stopping to change direction.

The students also established long-term friendships with me and with each other. I found that they would stay in touch long after the quarter was over. It was an intense experience that forged a kind of alliance—a love for robots and their applications.

During the first offering of MRPL, we also scheduled an experiment that grew and evolved every year: Ethics Day. Each quarter, near the midpoint of MRPL, when the students had lost their shyness and engaged in vibrant classroom discussion, we spent a day diving into the ethical and moral responsibilities of a robotics engineer. What sort of work should robots do? What responsibilities do roboticists have to consider the social impact of their inventions? Should robots make decisions to kill people in police or wartime action?

The Ethics Day conversation became a permanent fixture in every class I would teach for the ensuing thirty years; and the way students responded to these questions over the decades and through major milestones such as 9/11, became my proxy for how society's relationship to technology, morality, and warfare shifted over the years.

My funding, at the start of my career, came from the Department of Defense. That source, combined with the fact that the First Gulf War was part of my earliest adult experience, led me to an opt-out thanks to an incredibly understanding and responsive professor. That sequence of events led me to Educational Robotics, Ethics and Robotics, and a lifetime of research, all in a domino adventure that I never could have guessed four years earlier as I raced across the country in a solar-electric car.

As I was busily working on educational robotics and on outdoor robot navigation, my friends in the doctoral program, along with their faculty, were navigating a very different world where they would invent and participate in the first, great dot-com boom.

It started, as many things do, very small-scale, with research questions about online services. As soon as it became clear that computers around the country could be connected, we fell naturally into thinking of this large network of computers as a network of skilled technicians, like people. Can this society be engineered to function well together—to solve problems through collaboration? This became one strong current of thought about the new Web.

In addition, over the past decade AI researchers had already developed Agent Theory, formalizing just how an information-wielding and decision-making system could be thought of in terms of inputs, outputs, and internal memory. It was a short step to marry agent-based thinking with the nascent World Wide Web, suggesting a future in which each computer on the network hosted intelligent agents that could provide services to other agents in the network. One agent might provide weather forecasts. Another might help price flight tickets. Yet another might provide translation services between metric and imperial units. We humans would be just another sort of agent, coming in and recruiting this network of talents to solve our problems.

At the university, we worked on an architecture for these intelligent agents to interoperate. How would one agent in Michigan advertise that it can compute average salaries by occupation—in a language that all digital agents across the U.S. would understand? And how would another agent in Boston that tracked wind velocities tell all the other computers about its capabilities? Multiple research groups developed languages for asking questions, offering services, and even conducting barters so that there would be added value for all cooperating agents in the new digital society.

As these research concepts developed, the internet boom launched like a rocket ship. Multiple groups, each with their designs for just how intelligent agents should collaborate, began spinning out of the university, forming companies that attracted massive funding from the Silicon Valley venture capitalists, who were absolutely in love with this brand-new technology. I saw research groups rent asunder by competing startups; and some doors in the hallways of Computer Science closed, either because of "stealth" startups, or because some graduate students and some faculty simply became unavailable as they poured their time into new startup ventures fueled by Sand Hill Road.

Within months, these same startup companies began to be purchased outright by the biggest corporations who saw this as the future of the internet—and people that had been faculty and students with average income levels became millionaires overnight.

This initial phase of the dot-com boom changed the university, and it also changed the people. The materiality of massive financial gain influenced student aspirations. Some of the best, natural student-teachers around me gave in to join corporations—and this led to a very real loss of teaching talent that I believe took its toll for more than a decade. Some professors simply checked out of teaching and research, becoming swept up in a new gilded promise of extreme wealth, power, and the excitement of having direct impact on the future of a newly technologized society.

Intentions were good but also naïve—"We are going to revolutionize all communities; we are going to make all information available to everyone, for free!"—and materialistic. I had one friend who became, literally, worth one billion dollars. And he started just dreaming of what he would do with that money—except that the lockout clause restricting him from selling stock lasted right through to the dot-com collapse, rendering his billion dollars of equity worthless before he ever realized a dollar.

I also witnessed how wealth influenced each person I knew. Some purchased red Ferraris—really. Others purchased massive homes, in multiples. Others changed not one ounce. I watched one person drive their same, old car; wear their same old watch; and on the sly, purchase and land-grant the foothills toward the ocean to environmental nonprofits so that they could be shielded from development—all anonymously.

By the final year of my doctoral program, even I cofounded a company, Blue Pumpkin—but it was a software company, not a dot-com. That adventure further exposed me to the angel funders, venture capitalists, and culture of Silicon Valley—in that is an entire book all on its own.

Yet my primary work, day by day, was to finish my doctoral thesis, and to refine and teach our Mobile Robot Programming Lab. My love of teaching only expanded even as the dot-com storm around me swept so many people up and took them to an entirely different plane.

By the end of my doctoral career, it was clear that I faced two distinctly different possible futures—become a professor and commit to teaching; or stay in Silicon Valley and join the dot-com revolution. It was time for another dose of my futureproofing formula, and so I played my mind game. I applied to faculty positions, only securing a single interview in a single school, Carnegie Mellon's Robotics Institute; and at the same time, I continued my Blue Pumpkin company work, convinced that I could happily stay full-time and become an engineering lead at a growing software corporation.

I interviewed at Carnegie Mellon, and the week after, I hosted a conference at Stanford that was attended by some of the professors from CMU that had interviewed me. In the stairwell of the Computer Science Department, during one of the coffee breaks, I mentioned to one of the CMU professors that I was excited to receive their decision and he told me that they would not be offering me the job. I had done badly in the interviews, and he was disappointed. I had no time to process that backchannel, because I was running the conference. So I cocooned myself in the work at hand.

The next week, as I confidently prepared for my business future, I found myself sitting in my shared office with a Pittsburgh t-shirt on—one that I received as a gift from my brother, who had lived there. I talked to my officemate about how I would *not* be going to Pittsburgh. So, he bet me I would in fact become a professor at CMU—and he taped a single ruble to the door of our office to represent the bet. That same day, the Director of the Robotics Institute called me and said he was coming to Stanford and wanted to visit me and talk about my application.

When he arrived at my university, I brought him to our floor where I had set up a giant cardboard maze in the foyer with robots ready to run the very best Vader that any of our students had ever created. The robots moved smoothly, collaborating and picking up every piece of gold scattered in the maze; and I described to the director that this was all the work of undergraduate students in their very first robot programming class. He was impressed. It was educational robotics, not research, that convinced him to hire me.

Chapter 10

I Have Two Daughters

My generation remembers where we all were on 9/11. I was teaching class—only my ninth-ever class—at Carnegie Mellon to a roomful of undergraduates: Mobile Robot Programming Lab. We were discussing control and feedback systems for robots to maintain their balance as they careened through cardboard mazes. Police ducked into the room and told us class was over, and I headed to the conference room, where we congregated to look at the television report.

As a pilot, watching the first of the towers burning, all I could think about was how impossible it was for a pilot to make a mistake like that. I knew too much to hypothesize the "how," and none of us could have imagined in those first few minutes that it was deliberate. The second crash shifted the world under our feet.

In the early weeks and months, as an American, I was proud to see the entire world share our grief and promise to unite with us against a threat this heinous. It seemed as if the terrorists' intentions had entirely backfired; rather than making the United States seem weak, they succeeded in making the global community seem strong, united, clear-headed.

It was not even five months later that this goodwill and the emotions of an immigrant like me took a chaotic turn. President Bush gave his infamous speech, referencing 9/11 directly and then announcing the Axis of Evil: Iran, Iraq, North Korea. The terrorists had primarily Saudi passports; we would learn later of Bin Laden hiding in Afghanistan. But Iran? Iraq? North Korea? These countries all had autocratic, violent regimes, true. Just like a dozen other countries around the world. And, just like those other countries, we already knew they had nothing to do with 9/11.

This move backfooted the immigrant community—we were jolted from "multicultural" Americans sharing in grief to suspicious immigrants, and I saw this cracking of American unity in our everyday interactions. At Carnegie Mellon, we had Indian and Sikh colleagues who were verbally assaulted at the local grocery store in Pittsburgh while buying fresh vegetables. I received multiple calls from the FBI, leading to a long, in-person interview in my office with two agents. "Do you have contact with people in Iran? Do you have family there? Do you have friends there? Do you attend mosque? Are you aware of anti-American conversations in Pittsburgh? In California? When are you leaving the country next? Where are you going?" They left me their business cards. I kept one of them—it was fancy. It had a full-color, embossed FBI logo on it that showed significant relief from the thick cut paper.

The drumbeat of war against Iraq gained momentum over the year, and I returned to my critical examination of the press just like last time. All my nerves damaged by the First Gulf War in 1990 flared brightly again twelve years later.

I continued teaching at CMU, and I kept inserting an Ethics Day discussion in the syllabus for every course. In Ethics Day, I distributed discussion questions on the role of advanced technology in warfare— and whether robots should ever be given the agency to decide whom to kill.

The changes in student attitudes were stark. Before the Iraq War, the classroom would settle into a robust debate, with two strong positions espoused, each by at least a third of the class. One side would argue that other countries would no doubt embrace every technological advance for warfare, and therefore if we were to artificially avoid new technology, we would be at an unacceptable disadvantage. The other side would argue that the agency for war making needs to stay with people, because taking a life is irreversible and solemn.

The two sides would eventually find a compromise along the lines of universal regulations that all countries should be convinced to accept. Under these conditions, most would agree that we ought to keep autonomous robots out of war, but only if we can avoid disadvantaging the United States.

During the Iraq War, the discourse on Ethics Day changed—it flattened into a non-event. Nearly everyone would agree, at the outset, that the world faces a never-ending march of technological progress in war. Students would point out that autonomy and robotics are ill-conceived words. Cruise missiles have been around for decades, and they're nearly autonomous robots.

The press had taken pains to describe eyewitness accounts of such missiles literally flying above the streets of Baghdad, turning intersections almost magically, deftly avoiding schools, and then exploding upon contact with administrative buildings. The questions I was asking, students would point out, are essentially irrelevant; technology progresses, and we will always see it in war. The policy we need to have is simple: use whatever we can, because we are on the right side of justice.

Once P.W. Singer published *Wired for War* in 2009, I included readings from his analysis of robotics in warfare, pointing out his stories regarding how every advanced technology we develop for warfighting will be copied by our enemies within a decade. Singer's stories and analysis changed the tone of the debate gradually; and it was about ten years after 9/11 that I noticed Ethics Day returning to its ancestral roots, with a robust and balanced debate.

The thesis, however, had shifted. Students stopped speaking about the policy question of whether AI autonomy should be used in warfighting. Instead, the students began to explore a much more personal, career-oriented question: what should *my* role be in advancing AI and robotics research? What should I do with the lifetime of invention that is ahead of me?

Here, I saw a wisdom in the 2010s that was, and continues to be, the source of my optimism about the youngest generation of graduates entering the workforce. These recent students harbor a cynicism toward the concept of generating marginal profits for a mega-corporation to make tons of money. Their interest in massive material gain has dwindled, along with their interest in the concept of "privacy is dead."

Instead, they are seriously concerned. They are worried about democracy, loss of privacy, hate-speech online, polarization, and violence worldwide. They are dumbstruck by the elder generation's complete failure at taking stock of climate change—environmentally triggered mass migration, nutritional deficiency, political instability. They see us as having entirely lost the plot, and they want their lifetime of work to add up to Something Better.

In the years of the Iraq War, I also began engaging in discussions with my colleagues, faculty at Carnegie Mellon, about the ethics of robotics in warfare. In these years, some articles in the press began noting that I, and a few other faculty, were refusing Department of Defense funding for moral reasons, concentrating our innovation on pro-social technologies.

Faculty within my department began speaking with me about my attitude, and how I raised CREATE Lab funding. One professor, whose laboratory was funded to improve autonomous triggering systems for landmines, was genuinely baffled by my stance, and we had several discussions on whether and how making landmines "safer" made the world a better place or created more excuses to distribute even more mines.

I remember one discussion clearly, because it was borne out of a faculty member's strong desire to understand just why I was behaving the way I was. He helpfully drove me to the airport so we would have time to talk before a long trip. He played a Cat Stevens CD in his car—we are both of a generation that locks into his words. And he asked about my stance on war, research, and robotics. I explained that my attitude centered on opportunity cost. If I work on a research project, I want to actively acknowledge the projects I am choosing *not* to work on, and I want to be sure that the trade I have made is the one I can defend.

I explained that I wish to spend my career working on innovations that I hope are used immediately and broadly—not innovations that I hope are never needed because they are tools of violence and death. I explained that in my classes, I was not being prescriptive to the students. I just wanted them to understand this form of reflection—that whatever they choose to work on, they ought to choose it actively, with the confidence that they are choosing what's right for them.

He listened attentively, and here is how he disagreed. He said, "I have two daughters. The world is a dangerous place, and I will do anything to protect them. Anything."

His message stuck with me over days and years, because it shatters my reasoning style. In the rhetoric of ethics, there is an argument type called value hierarchy. Take something questionable that you are attempting to justify to others. Instead of directly defending it, place it alongside something clearly more heinous. The two issues do not even need to be directly related. But by fronting something despicable, you can dizzy the listener into winnowing their concerns. Say you are anti-immigration, and the public is concerned that illegal immigrants with children are being mistreated at the border. "You are worried about whether illegal immigrants have toothpaste in the holding shelters we place them in? Don't forget that those so-called parents stole children in Mexico so they could cross the border."

The more pedantic version of this, practiced by politicians frequently every year, is simply to provoke outrage about *anything*. That disarms any reasonable conversation even when, as is nearly always the case, the provocation is entirely shallow and caricatured.

The value hierarchy my colleague drew on me is shattering because there is no hope for me to change his mind. He honestly believes that his two daughters, the loves of his life, are endangered, and that whatever wars we instigate in the Middle East are in the service of protecting his daughters. Anything I say to him about harming human beings in the Middle East will only suggest to him that I wish to offer up his daughters for sacrifice, in the name of something like "a chance for goodwill and peace." Every moderating thought I attempt to provide will challenge the right of his daughters to live and to thrive.

The conversation is honestly lost before it has begun, and with that loss, so much else evaporates from the possibility of discussion:

Gone: War is systemic and the violence we wreak upon Iraq will come back to haunt us by creating hatred toward our politics and our power, and by becoming the rhetorical ammunition of extremists who want us to do exactly this.

Gone: The way we kill and the way we communicate regarding war-fighting demonstrates that we are caricaturing and dehumanizing the "other"—and this is a total failure of moral leadership.

Gone: The Iraqis had zero to do with September 11; why does that attack justify destroying the quality of life of tens of millions of civilians in a country that is irrelevant to the attack?

Gone: The world is not a dangerous place. It is a beautiful place, full of love and generosity. If you visit Iraq, or Iran, you will find gracious people who readily invite you to their home for a meal. Really.

Gone: Even if you wish to protect your daughters, all data analysis will suggest that every statistically legitimate chance of danger visited upon your daughters has nothing to do with Iraq, or even the entire Middle East.

All these potential discussions are dead on arrival because he has already permanently affixed the safety of his daughters in relation to Iraq. Anything I say against the war is a cruel invitation to expose his daughters to risk.

When FBI agents ask you if you communicate with anyone in Iran—as if this is suspicious activity for an Iranian-born American; when your colleagues connect the safety of their children to bombings in Baghdad; when the language of war reporting obviously dehumanizes people that have my same religion—all of this creates a chasm between your inner feelings and how you decide all the straight, conventional Americans around you must be feeling.

This period of war did not make me feel more Iranian. It made me feel both less American and less Iranian—like an alien stuck on an inhospitable planet where, thanks to my light complexion, most of the locals could interact with me without even realizing that I am such a complete outsider.

I will say there was one ray of light that always touched me, from the First Gulf War forward. I love to drive, and in driving through town, even during the Iraq War, I would weekly pass the intersection of Craig and Fifth Avenue in Pittsburgh. Without fail, a small band of elders, mostly women, would be holding their "Stop the War" signs, waving and smiling broadly. I always, always honk like a crazy person through these intersections—it is my small shout-out. The women look up and point, smiling, as I drive. And even if they do not know my reasons exactly, the very fact that they, through their many years, have come to the recognition that war cannot be trusted—I take solace in that as I deliver my weekly dose of honking.

Chapter 11

Iwan's Open Source

I regret to inform you that Iwan and his wife Catherine were killed in a severe car accident during a vacation on the West Coast on July 4. Iwan and Catherine were very much in love and were bright stars of kindness and intellect. Their loss is felt painfully.

Please direct any personal email to the Ulrich family. You can reach them at the following email address: e.ulrich@bluewin.ch. Please direct any email in regards to Iwan's projects at CMU to Illah Nourbakhsh, Iwan's advisor, at illah@ri.cmu.edu. I am sorry to bring you this bad news through such an impersonal medium.

Let this website and Iwan's other associated websites stand as a memorial to a life full of projects that have helped and touched many. In that our success in life is defined by the positive impact we have on those around us, Iwan is a model to whom all of us should aspire. The rest of this home page remains as Iwan left it, untouched.

Illah Nourbakhsh
The Robotics Institute

July 4, 2000. I was living temporarily in Lausanne, Switzerland, on sabbatical to co-author a textbook, *Introduction to Autonomous*

Mobile Robots. I had been invited out by my old solar race car colleague who was now a Professor at EPFL, the Swiss technical university near Geneva. I remember the tiny, one-room, temporary bedroom that I was using during my time because it came after an adventure.

Originally, I got off the train in central Lausanne, and right next to the railroad tracks was the original housing that had been arranged for me. I went in to find a hallway that looked exactly like a hostel: one shared bathroom/shower, and a whole lot of clothes on the floor, in the hallway, with many mattresses piled into a few bedrooms and a whole lot of pot in the air. I called EPFL in a panic. Now, here I was, in a private one-room studio that was well above threshold.

My phone rang in the witching hour, and the Dean of Students at Carnegie Mellon introduced himself to me. The reason for his call was the very worst reason you can possibly imagine. My first doctoral student at Carnegie Mellon, Iwan, who was in fact from a tiny Swiss rural village, had been vacationing at the Grand Canyon with his wife on a great American road trip. A truck had crossed the median and they had a head-on collision. Iwan and his wife did not survive.

The relationship between a professor and his doctoral student is unique. Over the course of years, you meet weekly, and you begin with an imbalance: the professor has knowledge, projects, a busy schedule; the student has new courses, unfamiliarity with the subject, and eagerness. Over the years, your relationship evolves from mentor-mentee to colleagues on equal footing. The student becomes a world expert in his area; he becomes busier and busier with research plans, conferences, meetings; and the professor is along for the ride, learning about the nuances and advances in the area from his student.

I had already made this transition with Iwan, over three years of weekly interaction. When we first met, he introduced himself with pictures of his beautiful Swiss mountain village, with a traditional dinner cooked by him and his wife for me, and with a steady stream of the very best Swiss chocolates. We were colleagues and friends, and I learned more from him, consistently. He was kind; he asked everyone in the Institute about their children, by name. He warmed the room when he entered.

The process of grief is sharp when a young one passes away. In Farsi, we use a specific word for this form of loss; when your child dies, we say that you burn. The metaphor is precise. A third-degree burn leaves a scar that is lifelong. In universities, our students are our academic children; and I was burned.

I have found in my half-century that, for each person that I lose, there are unique ways in which I process their loss and recover from grief, over time. In this case the date of his death—July 4—created a double meaning. As a small child, I adored fireworks—I was the type of child who would happily spend four hours parked along the road near Worlds of Fun in Kansas City to make sure the fireworks show would absolutely fill the sky. But the Iran-Iraq war made Independence Day complex, because my cousin from Iran, who was in Teheran when the bombs fell, associated the explosive sounds of fireworks with the sound of bombs falling around him. He reminded me of this often, and it colored my thoughts whenever I heard the explosive sounds afterwards.

And now there was Iwan's July 4 tragedy. The iconic date makes the annual landmark of Iwan's passing unavoidable for me. Twenty years later, July 4 is just as strongly attached to this memory.

===

I also processed the day with a ritual in solitary remembrance of my former student. I am an amateur classical guitarist, and on that trip to Lausanne, I missed playing. I had found a decent, used nylon-string guitar in town and purchased it just a week earlier. When Iwan died, I searched my files for a piece that I would learn, in memory of him. I chose the Venezuelan waltz, "El Negrito" by Antonio Lauro, and I learned and memorized it in the park, in Lausanne, daily.

Today, when I pick up a guitar, this is the second warm-up piece I always play; and I reflect on what Iwan taught me with each performance. It will forever remain an emotional piece of music for me.

I returned to Pittsburgh to organize Iwan's robotic laboratory equipment and his digital content. Iwan had concentrated his undergraduate research on robotic aides for persons with impaired vision, and his work had been groundbreaking in suggesting that technology, developed in concert with a user community, could potentially have authentic real-world consequences on quality of life. He designed the GuideCane, a steerable cane that provided feedback to the user about where obstacles were located as she moved through indoor and outdoor environments.

At Carnegie Mellon, we turned our attention to visual navigation: how could an electric wheelchair track its location, indoors and outdoors, using nothing more than a video camera? If we could successfully track location, our thinking was that an electric wheelchair could provide a far more intuitive interface for activities such as: "Follow this hallway to the first left or navigate through the narrow doorway into the building." Particularly for electric wheelchair users with whole-body motor challenges, head-controlled joysticks can make tasks like this time consuming, occupying far longer and making the job of getting from one place to another arduous in the extreme.

At the turn of the millennium, a major challenge for such research was simply ingesting an analog video camera's series of pictures into a mobile computer mounted on the wheelchair so that the images can be processed and interpreted using computer vision algorithms. Back then, we used large circuit boards, frame grabbers, to capture image signals and hand them over to a computer's main memory banks. This was time-consuming, expensive, and required larger computers than we could mount on a mobile robot or wheelchair.

Just as Iwan began his research, industry was developing laptops and cameras that used a much higher-speed digital data sharing standard, called IEEE-1394, nicknamed "Firewire." Firewire was a game changer for computer vision. It enabled new video cameras with digital outputs to easily connect to small, portable computers far more appropriate for mobile applications.

As Iwan and I purchased and tested these new-generation cameras, we encountered a major obstacle—there were no software systems that enabled the camera's digital contents, routed through Firewire, to be read programmatically in real time so that a robot could access the information in software. Iwan developed the very first Firewire visual driver, a software library custom-designed for this very purpose.

At the time, I knew that he was creating an open repository of his new driver online; and I watched him use his own library with great success as our motorized wheelchair demonstrated the ability to navigate sidewalks on Carnegie Mellon's campus and our indoor hallways, offices, and laboratories. We even tested the system in Iwan's home, and it was perfectly able to discriminate each and every room in their apartment. This was my context in which a generous and promising young gentleman was taken away from us—one who had developed a whole new driver, developed brand-new visual navigation systems, and who had shown a personal generosity toward me that made every interaction a joy.

When I returned to Pittsburgh, the university gave me editorial access to Iwan's web page, and I began by posting, at the very top, the difficult news for his visitors (reprinted verbatim at the head of this chapter), while preserving the rest of his web site for posterity.

To my surprise, I immediately began receiving, on my personal email account, dozens of tributes to Iwan by engineers from around the world. Some hailed from major businesses, including Intel Corporation and Hewlett Packard; others were hobbyists and researchers in computer vision and robotics from every corner. The university also gave me access to Iwan's email, so I could answer requests and gently complete interactions in his inbox. This is when I began a new voyage of discovery, seeing evidence of his incredible community engagement.

I saw researchers and hobbyists alike writing to Iwan, and in many cases writing to him knowingly posthumously, describing his kindness. Iwan had openly published his entire vision driver for Firewire; but that is just the very beginning of the story. He had forged direct, mentoring relationships with hundreds of users around the world. They described how he helped them customize their use of his software library; how he helped problem-solve each of their application prototypes; how motivated they were by his decision to innovate specifically to empower those who are marginalized in society.

In that decade, it was simply unimaginable for me to see this level of worldwide sharing facilitated by a first-year or second-year doctoral student. To see Intel Corporation researchers writing about how critical his software and his help was to their research progress—this was way outside the universe of possibilities that we could have expected from a young student in 1999.

I began adding up statistics on unique email messages from users of his library who went to the trouble to thank him so deeply—in his inbox and in my inbox alike. The numbers swelled beyond two hundred. How could a student who had been incredibly productive in his research efforts also simultaneously reach out, respond to, and mentor so many with his free, published software?

My deep dive into his second life showed me the value of opensource programming ethics in terms that I had never sufficiently appreciated. Iwan also opened my eyes to the possibility of downstream consequences: that our work holds value and not just because of the inherent value of what we actively choose to enact. Our work also builds value because it infuses others' future work with the values and goals that we embody in our initial launch.

Iwan, in a few short years, had accomplished an unimaginable amount of downstream, prosocial consequences by creating a tool attached to a philosophy of value-oriented invention that influenced his notably large user community. If we consider the impact of our decisions this fully, then our research and publication decisions become even more consequential, extending beyond the value of our own opportunity for enacting good with the more global scope of influencing public dialogue about the relationship of innovation to society.

My laboratory at Carnegie Mellon was originally called the Mobile Robot Programming Lab. Our ethos was defined in the negative: accept no military funding. But with Iwan's passing, and my awakening to our potential for impact, my lab came together and changed its name and its charter.

The Community Robotics, Education and Technology Empowerment lab (CREATE) became our name and our mission. Still, we would refuse military funding and violence-oriented research. But our underlying message became a positive one: find communities of practice, forge long-term, trusting relationships with them, and co-design technological interventions that empower practitioners to enact their values.

Two decades of CREATE efforts have forged relationships around the world. If we count the dozens of CREATE staff efforts over that time, it adds up to more than four hundred person-years of community-engaged work. All this, inspired by three years with young Iwan Ulrich.

Chapter 12

What Did You Do This Morning?

The beginning of the twenty-first century brought forth a period of relative calm, but not before the gauntlet of Y2K. A few of us on the university's campus received special Y2K badges, licensing us to stay on campus, on call, as the clock struck midnight on December 31, 1999. I am still not entirely sure what we were to do if all the computer servers had failed in that instant. As it turned out, we sat in our offices, counting the minutes until possible technological Armageddon, watching New Year's Eve celebrations from around the world, and nothing at all happened. The calm after the storm lasted, right from Y2K, until September 11, 2001, twenty months later.

I was a new professor those years, so my every waking hour was filled with anxiety about one basic question: where would I get funding? This is the lot of new researchers in the United States. We spend all our energy finding a job at a university, then we discover that the university is a hands-off vessel for our work, not a benefactor. Our job, once hired, is to design and teach classes, and then to keep the job by doing world-class research forever. But to do the research, we need to consistently recruit and pay graduate students as well as several months of our own summer salary—all of which depends on constant fundraising—for decades. It is just like being a Silicon Valley entrepreneur, constantly on the prowl for money—except that we don't own explosively growing companies, we cannot pitch wealthy venture capitalists, and we cannot become millionaires.

During this phase of funding anxiety, I received a cold call from a colleague at the Robotics Institute. "Illah, how would you like to build a robot for a museum? Inside Dinosaur Hall, at the Carnegie Museum of Natural History? The director over there wants a robot. There's funding. And he asked three of us here at CMU and we've all said no. So do you want the job?"

After swallowing that I had just been told I was the fourth choice, I immediately said yes and began what has turned into a lifelong friendship with the museum's director. Together, we built a robotic guide that could take museum visitors on a tour of the lesser-visited exhibits in Dinosaur Hall. The combination of Jurassic era dinosaurs and space age robotics felt like both a perfect form of irony and also pure candy for children visiting the museum: dinosaurs and robots.

The excitement of this work was overshadowed right away by my first taste of university politics during the first month on the project. One of the professors who had turned down the project visited my office unannounced and told me to stop. He said that the money was insufficient, and I should quit now, and that if I didn't stop, it would ruin my career. He said, point blank, that he would be in the room when I was up for promotion and tenure. I remember my naïve answer: "That makes no sense; I want to do the project; goodbye." For someone who hates being judged, the reminder that politics were in play and my future was subject to the whims of my colleague colored my sense of belonging at the university for years to come.

We pushed forward and recruited two outstanding Swiss students, even starting a small company to bring two Bay Area programmers from my undergraduate days east for work outside of regular tech programming. The museum's education division cut informational videos that the robot presented to visitors on laserdisc. That's right, a giant, spinning laserdisc player sat in the belly of our robot in the year 2000. A theatre stage fabricator at CMU designed and built the seven-foot-high steel robot body, which reflected the heritage of Pittsburgh in steelmaking and welding.

The robot navigated Dinosaur Hall using a video camera that trained on colored squares placed high on the walls of the cavernous space, and even plugged itself into the wall nightly to recharge and prepare for the next day's work. To keep this complex system running, we wired a paging system into the robot's body, and my Swiss students and I took turns wearing a pager, just like E.R. doctors. The idea of being on-call for a museum robot was both exciting and ridiculous.

At any hour of the day or night, my pager would buzz with a message like: "I'm lost, and my battery is dying." I would jump up from the dinner table at a restaurant, sprint to my car, drive to the museum as if I was in an ambulance, and then use my pass to get into the museum. I would run down the halls, pull a cart out of a broom closet—a cart that contained a keyboard and television monitor—and wheel it over to the broken robot to plug it in, so I could understand just what had gone wrong before its internal batteries died.

Sitting in the museum at midnight with a Tyrannosaurus Rex towering over me, nearly all the lights off, and tapping away on my keyboard—it felt like my dreams had come true. Later, I would do additional robot installations at the Smithsonian Air and Space Museum and at the San Francisco Exploratorium. The rush of being in a museum after closing time, and belonging there, never grows old.

Three events during these sweet four years of museum robotics deeply influenced my thinking about technology and society. The first story involves a pattern we noticed in the first year of the robot's deployment. We would receive emergency pages from the robot and race to find it, its battery draining, unable to plug into the wall—and we would notice that the museum lights had been turned completely off. We could tell what time this happened because of the robot's logs, and since it used a camera to find the plug, darkness blinded it entirely. The lights were being turned off by someone before the robot had parked, and it was consistently about an hour earlier than they were supposed to be switched off.

I started talking to the security guards and the docents—volunteers who loved to interact with children at the museum and take them on tours of Dinosaur Hall—that I had never spoken to in all these months of programming, engineering, and testing at the museum.

I learned that I had been an arrogant engineer. I had invaded the museum with fancy equipment, with students, and with a technology that was basically absurd. I had created a tour guide robot, costing hundreds of thousands of dollars, in a context where volunteer docents took great pride in providing tours to children daily, for free. They felt rightly threatened by my technological toy. Why on earth would I use a robot to replace the work of caring, human docents who aren't even paid? They were angry, and they repeatedly told me that I was there to replace them.

Chastened, my students and I began to befriend the docents, and we asked them to help us design the robot's new educational content. We showed the docents how to select laserdisc media content on the robot and changed our approach so that the docents were in control and the robot was their assistant. They would chat with children, talk about various topics, then use the robot to play their selected video content, even telling the children all about the robot and its inner workings.

The power relationship was rebalanced as it should have been; but I had come into this space blind, waving my electronic wand with no regard for the culture and feelings of people already in the space. That would change how I allowed my technologies, in future years, to be inserted into social and cultural relationships.

The second story started with a message left for me on my office phone by one of our now friendly security guards from the museum. *"Your robot is drunk."* I checked the robot's computer logs remotely and saw nothing wrong. I remember sitting in my office at Carnegie Mellon, deciding this was not a high priority, but at some point, I ought to walk over there and see what the joke was about.

When I made my way to the museum a day later, I was stunned by what I saw. Entering Dinosaur Hall, our robot, with several children in tow, was meandering down the hallway. Meandering, serpentine style. It would jerk left, roll toward one edge of the hall, then gradually turn right until it was headed in the right direction, only to overshoot, jerk left again, and repeat.

I paused the robot and got down on my hands and knees to look at the robot's wheels. It had four wheels, and each metal wheel had a thick rubber tire wrapped around its outer edge. One rubber tire had come completely off its wheel, and this caused two mechanical problems. First of all, the robot was teetering because the metal wheel would catch and one of the other three working wheels would lose contact entirely. What's worse, when the metal wheel spun against the marble floor of the museum, it had no traction at all, and the robot would slip like a car on ice.

But this robot did not navigate by paying attention to its wheel slip at all. It navigated visually, with a camera mounted seven feet high, by staring at giant, colored squares at the end of the hall. The computer would command the robot to go straight, and it would veer left. The computer would see the visual landmark slipping to the right in its camera view and command the robot to turn right to stay on track.

This cat-and-mouse game between slipping wheels and obsessive visual navigation constantly played out, resulting in a very drunk robot. Yet the robot never hit the wall, and never noticed its own folly. As long as its logs were concerned, it could see the landmarks and was navigating just fine on some presumably horrible terrain. It never detected any anomalies on its own and never paged us.

I was fascinated by the fact that the robot was partly broken but was unintentionally compensating for its own problem. I had always thought of robots as fragile machines that either work or fail, occupying a simple binary. I thought of humans as creatures that can have aches, pains, problems, and constantly function in the gray area of being partly alright and partly broken.

But the complexity of the machines we were building now far exceeded that of robots even a few years earlier. They were so multifaceted that they were no longer in the binary space of working or broken. They could be anywhere in the spectrum in between—working, sort of; failing, a bit. I began to study other machines and found that this trend was not isolated: as we have created ever more complicated systems around us, we have introduced more nuanced forms of failure that we cannot easily test for, and worse yet, we cannot consistently predict or detect.

Examples of system complexity and its unintended consequences are numerous, from superfast computerized options trading to the Boeing 737 SuperMax autopilot. But in 2010, the example that I digested and began consistently using in my classes was that of the Toyota Prius brake failure.

News stories had begun publishing accounts of Prius owners who complained that they stepped on the brakes, the car didn't slow down right away, and this totally surprising response resulted in a fender bender.

Toyota, like all car companies, began by suggesting that user error was to blame—just as Audi had blamed Audi 5000 drivers years earlier: "If the car is violently accelerating when put in drive, then it must be the drivers who are confusing the accelerator pedal with the brake."

Toyota also suggested user error, as if somehow users began mistaking the brake and accelerator pedals all at once, everywhere. The Prius problem was finally uncovered by none other than Steve Wozniak, one of the founders of Apple Computer, who subjected his car to a range of conditions and discovered that the chips in the antilock braking system had been programmed incorrectly, such that a particular amount of vibration would cause the ABS to stop braking. The problem was incredibly rare as far as a single car is concerned. But when you have millions of cars on the road, a rare event still happens dozens of times a month.

The underlying problem, which I started to understand from my drunk robot experience, is system complexity, combined with two other special ingredients: the hubris of engineers who think more technology is always better; and the naiveté of users, reporters, and regulators, who think the engineers are infallible.

We live in a world with ever-increasing technological complexity. The technologies around us will make more and more decisions for us. Yet as they become more entangled with our lives, their complexity makes it harder and harder for engineers to be *sure* that they will behave properly in rare circumstances.

We cannot, during testing, subject a Prius prototype to every condition it might face when millions are on the road. We cannot think up and test every failure of an aircraft system, or robot system, because we don't know what we don't know.

When I began to question so-called smart bombs in the First Gulf War, I was aware that technology was casting an optimistic light upon a fundamental technologic limitation. But it was only as I became more personally involved in technology and real-world applications that I began to appreciate the degree to which every passing year has brought us more advanced technology, more inscrutable complexity, and more surprising failures and errors. This pessimistic view of technology's dangers, in excess, began to drive my books, lectures, and course curricula.

The third story of my museum robot career is the story of a single day of beltway politics, and it overhauled my understanding of government, policy, and public spending. During the heyday of our museum robot work, I received a call from the National Aviary—another museum in Pittsburgh that was interested in integrating a robotic tour guide into its space. They are a national museum, and so they reasoned that, with a robotic tour guide, they would be able to open their doors to schoolchildren in all fifty states for virtual explorations of their live birds. The Aviary and its board had a specific plan for finding the money to pull this off, and they asked me to show up at the Pittsburgh airport, at a specific location away from the commercial side, one weekday morning.

I drove to the address they specified, left my car, walked through a door into a private aircraft facility, out the other side, and up the tiny staircase of a Gulfstream business jet. The entire boarding process took about a minute. No boarding passes, no security, no metal detectors. The ease of that boarding process threw me totally off. I knew that travel, for the one percent, was easier. But is this much easier? It was convenient, yes; but it was also shocking, after years of ever-tightening security, to board an airplane with literally no pause.

Our first stop in Washington, D.C. was the office of a lobbying firm, where the Aviary's representatives and I were told exactly how the day would play out and what our roles were in each meeting. The day was scheduled to the minute, with meetings in the congressional offices of Republican and Democratic representatives and senators. The ordering of the meetings was precise, the lobbyists explained, because of how power is negotiated in Capitol Hill. We had to convince lower-echelon representatives first, while assuring them that we were not yet asking for their vote on the budget appropriation until their senior mentor and colleague was willing to play along. It was like a giant network of permission-granting that would fall into place, when set up, if triggered in exactly the right way—just like a row of dominoes.

The day was utterly striking in so many ways. Our song and dance in each office was the least interesting part, because it was a literal repeat a dozen times. The Aviary would talk about their birds, about their national responsibility to educate; then I would come in as the geeky CMU professor, talking about how we can use high-tech robotics to bring the Aviary to the whole nation through the magic of telepresence and the new internet highway system. But the responses of the representatives were exactly as the lobbyists had explained ahead of time. "Is Arlen on board? Is Nancy on board? Talk to Bob. If he's on board, and if Arlen's on board, then I'm on board." The meat of every conversation was about the network of people and their attitudes about this project; that, by far, overwhelmed any interest or curiosity about the educational goals or technological feats of the work.

Each office we visited was also strikingly unique. The House offices were old, small, and plain. When you walk into a motel and you are slightly disappointed by the halls, the furniture, and the walls—this was the feeling in the House.

There was also an obvious discrepancy between Democratic and Republican front office workers. The Republican offices greeted you with secretaries who looked like small variations on the same conventional theme: tall, white, blonde, long-haired women. Every one of them. The Democratic offices greeted you with staff who came in every skin color, in several cases with wheelchairs. The disparity between homogeneity and diversity was striking.

My strongest memory stems from what happened when we visited Senator Arlen Specter's office late in the day. His opinion on our project was at the hub of many of our politicians' hedges about whether to support funding for the project; so, nothing was more important than his decision that day. We were shown to a huge conference room, and we proceeded to wait some twenty minutes in awkward silence, wondering if we had been forgotten. A senior staffer finally came in, sitting across from us with his cadre of assistants in tow. He looked at us, and here is the first thing out of his mouth:

"I decided how to spend a billion dollars this morning. What did you do?"

That was the perfect icing for my adventure in Washington. The level of personal conceit and hierarchy that he demonstrated out loud was exactly what I was digesting just under the surface in every meeting we held. He was just self-centered enough and socially awkward enough to make it utterly obvious.

I wrote earlier about complexity in robot systems—just like the robot tour guides I was busy selling to Congress. But complex social machinery has surrounded us for much longer than robotics has. How else could we describe the successful effort to get Congressional funds for a robot in Pittsburgh? The decision-making process was not based on the quality of ideas; it was based on power, hierarchy and networks. The lobbying strategy I saw was a well-oiled machine that knows exactly how to exploit every gear in the system to conjure up a result—provided the customer knows the right people and pays the best lobbyists for that result.

I learned that day that funding is not genuine validation. Complex systems make mistakes, and we cannot often detect that mistakes have even been made. My robot tour guides taught me that the mistakes of complexity extend well beyond engineered systems and into the social contexts surrounding the use of technology. From drunk robots to cartoonish decision-making in Congress, we consistently fail to appreciate the ramifications of our own complex systems.

So, imagine my total disappointment in recent years as the world's technologists and reporters spend considerable time touting the benefits of autonomous, driverless cars. Cognitive tutors that would teach children math better than any teacher. Even smarter smart bombs that hover until they notice something suspicious, then autonomously choose a target, dive, and explode. AI doctors that look at patient's medical records, chat with the patient, and make recommendations that outperform human physicians. AI-based hiring systems that eliminate sexism from Fortune 50 companies because they are gender-blind. Every one of these ideas has been promoted as a triumph of technology, riddled with errors and, finally, subject to waning support today. They're just too complex.

Chapter 13

Training Camp

Introducing the TSA Terrorist Trap ™

1. *Anxiety: Put an inscrutable Sharpie mark on subject's landing card.*

2. *Surprise! Wait until the last second to pull subject out of line as they exit customs.*

3. *Vulnerability: Take subject's passport, driver's license, and any other I.D.*

4. *Steep the Tea: Subject should remain seated along a blank wall with zero contact for at least half an hour, while vulnerable.*

5. *Lie Detector: Call subject to the desk, then ask them ten questions with answers your computer already displays for you.*

6. *Paper Panic: Ask subject for proof of homeownership, residency, occupation—anything demanding paperwork that no one ever carries in their pocket during a trip.*

7. *Sports Quiz: Ask subject about the Steelers. If that goes well, pivot to baseball or hockey. Do not, under any circumstances, bring up soccer.*

8. *Deadpan Finale: Ask subject if they're a terrorist.*

Every immigrant who has lived here for decades spends much of their time in a self-constructed bubble, with friends and colleagues who almost never bring up the whole immigrant thing. It can fade from consciousness for days at a time. But the boundary moments are the exception, when we operate outside our constructed social networks and suddenly become immigrants again. For me, these boundary moments always happen during international travel, which I love—until the moment I step off the airplane at JFK or Newark and have to begin navigating reentry.

In the early 2000s, coming back from South Africa during a decade of regular visits gave me repeated exposure to the immigration process, each time a depressing episode subsequent to a wonderful, fulfilling journey in Cape Town and Johannesburg.

Here in the U.S., I am a minority by birth country and by my Muslim religion. I live in a place where the structures of power are firmly rooted in the hands of white, European-descent Americans. Just walking in a city like Cape Town—then visiting the seat of government in Pretoria—the evident power structures and majority are refreshingly different. Black South Africans have legitimate majority in national government; the Cape Malay residents of Cape Town run the town and the businesses. Islam is revered just as highly as Christianity—with "Happy Ramadan" signs even in the local Nando's chicken restaurants. There is zero history of conflict with Iran, and so my national roots elicit genuinely welcoming comments.

So, a week or two in South Africa, and my guard is entirely down. I feel like a normal member of a diverse community, and it is a pleasure. Yes, there is massive wealth inequity in the country, as well as racism and unbelievable concentration of capital ownership in the hands of white South Africans. Problems are numerous and structural. But as I walk down a street and interact with locals, I feel less isolated, less alien, than every day in Pittsburgh.

The time inevitably arrives that I have to head home; and anxiety builds first in the passport control line. I stand in the U.S. Citizens line, clutching my passport and landing card, wondering if it will be easy or hard today. The passport control station will take extra time as they pull up my information on their screen, but the interaction is superficial. When the officer hands my passport and landing card back to me, there is frequently an interesting mark on the card. A single letter, or a mathematical symbol. The next bit, standing and waiting for luggage to arrive off the conveyor belt, is mainly time spent making sideways glances at everyone else's landing cards. Find the most normal-looking white American family and see if they have '+' marks on their cards too. This is an exercise in trying to figure out how worried I should be about an interrogation before exiting to the arrivals lobby.

With my luggage in hand—which usually contains an insane number of jam jars from Africa, because their jam is that good—I wheel toward the "Nothing to Declare" customs exit line, where an officer wordlessly collects our landing cards. The sliding electric doors just beyond the officer mesmerize me. They are the doors to freedom. If I can reach those doors, I am back in the U.S. and free! I watch people go through the doors, stepping into freedom group by group. I reach the front of the line—and I have even tried handing the landing card over upside-down, in the hopes that my special mark will receive no attention. This is where the officer nicely asks me to step aside, and then delivers special instructions. "Go over there, to your right. Go down that hall. On your left there is a door marked 'D.' Go in that room."

The adventure begins. As I walk to Door D, I have a recurring fantasy. Maybe they know I'm a roboticist and they want my help with an exciting space mission. Maybe they know I would be on this flight, and this is the President's way of finding a secure location to chat with me and recruit me.

It has never worked out that way. Door D leads to a ten-foot square room with a row of chairs and a few bank-style teller windows. Usually the entire thing is empty, and so when I enter, I stand there, luggage in hand, wondering how loudly to say "Hello?"

The agent that shows up beckons me, takes my passport, and says, "Do you have a driver's license?" I hand that over, too, and he tells me to have a seat. He turns and disappears with my documents. End of story.

It is a strange feeling to sit in the chair there, in some sort of no-man's-land. I am not in the U.S. exactly. But I've left Africa. And I have no identity documents on me any longer—nothing. It feels naked and uncertain, and there is nothing to do but check the time and begin waiting, wondering if the flight connection from New York to Pittsburgh is an utterly lost cause.

When I finally do get called back up to the window, a new officer asks a series of questions that move through a near-identical script. First, there are the questions I call "Lie Detectors," because they are all questions for which they surely have all the answers. Real-life examples:

"How long have you lived here? How many days were you away?"

"Do you have any family in Iran? Do you ever contact them? Do you ever email people in Iran? Do you ever call them?"

I remember the family questions—because they look ever more concerned as I answer yes to questions that are implicitly asking whether I love my family. "Yes, I contact my family in Iran." "Yes, I call them. I write to them." "That's right, I talk to them regularly. All the time." "Yes, I've visited them. They're, like, my family." "Yes. Yes, they visit me. Did I mention that they're my family?" Perhaps, for Iranians who have been disowned by their family, or where excommunication runs rampant, they get a shortcut pass out of interrogation at this point.

"Where do you work? Where do you live?"

The work questions give me a chance to turn the tables a little bit. I try to throw in the words "Professor" and "Robotics" as early as possible in the answers. "I make robots. I study the effects of technology on society. I lecture on how robots reinforce hegemonic power structures—how they make governments and large corporations more powerful." I love using "hegemonic", "power," and "government" in the same sentence on them. Sometimes this leads to a tiny crack: "My kid, he likes robots. He builds them out of Legos." I consider it a rip-roaring success when the agent says something like that.

Next, there are a series of questions about why I was away.

"What were you doing in South Africa?"

These are fun because I can milk my work details some more—my aim is to humanize myself as much as possible: "I taught a class on panoramic photography to schoolchildren in Soweto. I taught the same class in Cape Flats. I visited an Art Therapy school in a low-income neighborhood. I surfed on the Strand. I celebrated Christmas with my friends—you know what, it's summer there. So, for Christmas we had a barbecue on the beach."

Sometimes, the "Paper Panic" questions appear next. I do not have a good theory for what they intend to prove with these, because they are basically requests for paperwork that no one has.

"Do you have proof of residence?"

"Uh, my driver's license, which you have, has my address on it."

"No, do you have proof that you live here?"

"Like, what?"

"A utility bill or a credit card statement with your home address."

I remember one trip, where I was jumping for joy at this point—because I had to take utility bills with me to South Africa to open a local bank account; and so, I had all the paperwork sitting in my backpack. I took them out and proudly handed them over, expecting a thanks or a bravo. Neither was forthcoming.

"Also, do you have proof of employment?"

"Proof of employment? Like, what?"

"Do you have a letter from your employer stating that you work for them?"

"If you Google me, you can find my website at Carnegie Mellon. It's really clear."

"Do you have paperwork?"

"I have a business card. You want my business card?"
"Yes."

No joke—on one trip back, I handed over my driver's license, passport, two utility bills, a credit card bill, and a business card. That was my hole-in-one trip, where I had nearly everything they asked for in my backpack, by sheer luck.

The next bit is the "Sports Quiz"—to see if I am a total recluse in the U.S., or if I actually have basic party skills. And no matter where I land, from Atlanta to Newark, the officers always begin by asking me what I think of the Steelers.

Now, I am not a fan of football—quite the contrary. But I know to always read up on the Steelers before returning to the U.S., and it always pays off. I can usually express, with disgust, how much better they could be doing. And then if they switch to baseball, I can drone on about how unbelievably poor the Pirates' win-loss record has been. Being really angry about a sports team's mediocrity usually does it—it pops the interview out of the weeds, and they wish me well and say goodbye, handing over my documents.

However, on one trip back from South Africa, the officer took a beat after this line of questioning, then looked right at me and asked this zinger: "Were you at a training camp?" I thought, we've talked about the Steelers already. This can't be happening. I misheard.

"Excuse me?"
"Were you at a training camp?"

Well-intentioned folks reading this: you are probably thinking, "Umm, he's just wondering if you went to a training school for, say, sailing or lacrosse or something. You're reading too much into the question, Illah." And sitting there, listening to the officer ask this question, I will tell you it was impossible to genuinely understand his purpose. I can assure you now that he was not asking about sailing. He was asking if I had been at a terrorist training camp. And I suppose South Africa is so far away, he decided there might be terrorist training camps there.

The first impulse any normal person has, in this situation, is to pounce. "Are you kidding? You know all about me now—I'm a professor, and I worked at NASA before that, and you're asking me if I'm a terrorist in training really? And that's a DUMB QUESTION. Do some folks just say, 'Oh, yeah. Shit. You got me. I was at one, you're right!' I won't answer a question that stupid!"

But that is never what I say, because I want to be free, and back in the U.S. So, I answer this question with seriousness in my voice, and respect on my tongue. "No, sir. I was not."

And so far, in all my years, that's it. They hand back the documents, and they tell me I am free to go. I walk back to the main hall and finally get to exit through the electric sliding doors.

Small price to pay for freedom, right? After all, there are bad actors out there, and the fact that agents spent all that time with me should make me feel better, right? It means they are taking our American safety seriously. This is what some of my friends say, like justifying how I should embrace taking my shoes off in security because it makes us all safer.

But that is not how I feel. How I feel is alienated by a level of suspicion that is unjustifiable. And so, a few years ago, I did not walk out the electric, sliding doors after the agent said I'm free to go. I left the room angry about the training camp question, hesitated, and then I walked right back into Room D on my own. I told the agent that every time I come back to the U.S. I get this treatment. And it's ridiculous. Their computer knows me intimately by now—why the game? Who do I talk to in order to get this to stop?

The agent excused himself and came back with a form for me to fill out, along with a letter I was to write explaining everything. I took the time to fill out the formwork, wrote a multi-page letter on Carnegie Mellon letter-head, and sent it to the PO Box as instructed. That letter, against all odds, worked. Since that day, even after dozens of international arrivals, I have never been sent to Room D again.

Chapter 14

Shit Runs Downhill

Financial Anxiety
 Jealousy
  Regret
   Sulking
    Reflection
     Gratitude
      Acceptance

This is the emotional wave that I surf almost weekly, and it is powered by all the times I have brushed against entrepreneurial success, absurd wealth, and the hyper-confidence of the Silicon Valley way of life. The Silicon Valley version of the American Dream is popularly understood to be that a good, innovative tech idea will make the inventor rich. In the Bay Area, we used to say that, if you have a decent idea, shake the trees on Sand Hill Road and money will come pouring down. But the reality of this dream is, of course, as broken as the broader version of the American Dream nationally. The meritocracy of innovation that we subscribe to is poisoned irreparably by how privilege and existing wealth confer extreme advantage to a tiny proportion of innovators. If you can manage to jump on their train, then you, too, will become unfathomably wealthy. And if you miss the caboose, then your chances are marginal, no matter how honorable and innovative your idea may be.

The stew that cooks the Silicon Valley way is something that I began noticing in graduate school at Stanford, where the professors and students were, by large margins, well on their way to financial success, but at the same time were also ordinary human beings, teaching me and taking classes with me.

I transitioned from undergraduate to grad student as the First Gulf War finished and my activist friends and I talked nonstop about power, misinformation, and privilege. But within the bubble of my graduate school, I witnessed nearly zero emotional reaction in my classmates and teachers to the idea that hundreds of thousands of lives had just been ended, in war, without an honest moral accounting. Yet some of my stoic research collaborators were livid about something else: homelessness, poverty, and social safety nets.

I had endless debates with researchers about the misery around us—unhoused persons were visible in Palo Alto before the city pushed them further out. East Palo Alto, where some of us volunteered time, was literally across the highway before it became redeveloped into big-box stores. My colleagues were intent on convincing me that every person gets just what they deserve, that social care was a waste of time because it set up negative reinforcement cycles. They were convinced that anyone who works sufficiently hard will succeed, just as they had done themselves—many of them immigrants.

The statistical fallacy undergirding this intellectualized idea is rampant: I know someone who worked hard and succeeded in difficult circumstances. Therefore, people who don't make it are losers who do not want to succeed. The same fallacy infects the other end of the success scale: I know someone who had a good idea, got fifty million dollars, and is a billionaire now. Everyone who doesn't get that first fifty just doesn't have a good enough idea.

Of course, historical context, inequity, baked-in disadvantage—these are all missing from these discussions because my debate opponents are never, ever students of history. I have faced a billionaire who has asked me, mid-discussion: "What's that word mean that you just used: 'redlining?'"

The debates about our societal responsibility carried on, but I did not change my mind effectively. And the dot-com revolution drowned out these discussions as my colleagues began spinning out companies—validating their own beliefs that truly worthy souls will indeed succeed.

Their companies were initially organized around early versions of applied Artificial Intelligence for dot-com businesses, and they were quickly sold for hundreds of millions of dollars each. Just to be clear about the time scale—I am talking about researchers and young students at a university moving from idea to company to one hundred million dollars in the space of roughly eighteen months.

As my studies matured, I finally became caught up in startup culture myself, even as I was aiming for a life dedicated to university teaching and research. I became co-founder of a new company, Blue Pumpkin Software, and this gave me a front-row seat in watching just how wealth creation really happens the Silicon Valley way.

During a time of dot-com froth, we were the crazy founders who started a conventional software company. We sold ordinary working software for scheduling employees to conventional companies' call centers. Yet we visited the venture capital offices, made friends with the angel funders, and eventually raised capital and grew to more than a hundred employees.

The dot-com bubble burst eventually, and our little company carried on as the economy retracted and I began my professorship at Carnegie Mellon. My lesson in privilege and power negotiations came to a head when a much larger company finally agreed to purchase Blue Pumpkin for tens of millions of dollars. Up until that point, I had assumed that owning equity in a company matters—that the payout when a company is sold is based on stock ownership, and therefore all those employees would get the money to settle their mortgages and college debts.

But this is not at all what success looks like in the tech age. The investors in a company are God—they get to set the terms of their investment, and part of those terms are that they privilege their payout above all others. For example, they may give you a million-dollar investment for your company and take on ten percent ownership, but they will write the contract so that they receive triple their investment back before anyone else in the company gets a cent. Preferred stock. Guaranteed payout rates. The ten percent ownership concept is, honestly, a farce. This is the grammar of a special form of sensibility: "We are the titans with the money that you need; and by giving you our money, we are taking the most important position; therefore, we deserve the greatest benefit, even if anything goes south."

The investors always win—this is designed into the system; and there are privileged crumbs they distribute to company leadership. The CEO of the company receives a purse of money to distribute to whomever they wish to reward, including themselves, as a small fraction of the purchase price. This money, too, is not distributed based on equity or options or any other quantitative measure that is inclusive of all employees. Instead, the CEO distributes this money, with the absurd conflict of interest that every dollar given to someone else is a dollar less that they will take home.

At this point you may think this is a garden of the variously privileged— wealthy middle-class folks like me complaining about even wealthier upper-class people. But stop and think about the employees who join startups. Many of them are first-generation college graduates. They have worked hard to get a degree, and many are saddled with college debt because college is so obscenely expensive in our country. They may have a young family but have taken on this high-risk job with a lower salary because the company has offered them 0.1 percent ownership.

They keep thinking, "Well, if the company sells someday for fifty million dollars, then I will get three hundred thousand dollars after taxes—enough to pay off my college debt and half my mortgage." The employees are constantly doing this calculation as they see news of companies bought and sold left and right. And then their company sells for a hundred million dollars. And they get a twenty-thousand-dollar check, not a three hundred-thousand-dollar check. Twelve thousand dollars after taxes—out of one hundred million dollars.

In the years that followed, I helped many of my friends as they worked through investment deals and robotics companies. I began paying close attention to terms sheets and investment contracts and was regularly stunned to find the same game played every time, in every contract: investors saddle the company with the risk, and disproportionately maximize the profits for themselves. That is the real Silicon Valley version of the American Dream—a dream that ensures that wealth begets extreme wealth and weighs down everyone else, up and down the spectrum of privilege, with structural barriers against financial success.

So, peering into this world from just outside it, I was a happy professor in Pittsburgh. But the near misses with extreme wealth and prosperity continued to follow me. I remember walking in Palo Alto with my PhD advisor on one of my visits out west and running into Sergey Brin, one of the co-founders of a tiny company named Google, on his roller blades. I knew him from classes we shared, and he had started this little company and already grown it to about fifty employees. He pushed me to quit CMU and join his team right then and there. I politely declined. You do not forget an opportunity like that, nor the analysis and self-justification that you perform dozens of times thereafter—for instance, if I had joined his company, perhaps I would be a different person with different values, so it's all okay.

Years later, I was building a wooden seesaw in my Pittsburgh backyard when I received a call from the close friend of another Google founder: "Come join Project Chauffeur." The caller painted a picture for me of what the world would look like if every machine with a steering wheel was driven by a robot rather than a human. He kept repeating that we would save seventy thousand lives a year in the U.S. alone—because that is the number of people who die unnecessarily, every year, in single driver accidents. He also said that if Google could take on all the jobs that involved driving vehicles, that would be worth more than a trillion dollars of revenue. Just imagine: all the people who drive forklifts, taxis, buses, trucks, cars. Now transfer all their hourly paychecks to technology revenue at Google, which would own the replacement software that would displace all their driving jobs.

I had questions. What happens to tens of millions of workers? Isn't driving a social rather than mathematical act? Can AI really do this messy job with pedestrians, potholes, and baby strollers reliably enough, or do you just end up, like in airplanes, with a pilot and autopilot working together? Won't that be expensive because you haven't replaced the people? And if you do replace the people, what happens to them, their income, their family dependents?

The impatient answer to my question, which I heard for years on end, was simple: "What's the matter with you? Don't you want to save seventy thousand lives a year?"

There is that rhetorical flourish again, suggesting that a decision is obvious because of an artificial binary. My problem with his question is that we don't *know* that we will save lives each year. And we don't know how much damage we do to people when we shift labor economies massively. And we don't know how our technology is going to fail us when we make highly optimistic assumptions about our own future-facing capabilities.

So, I said no, right as I was using a sledgehammer to pound the seesaw stand into my grass yard and mixing concrete to surround it. That day, I finished the seesaw, and I stopped thinking about autonomous driving, years before the public face of driverless car companies, experiments, and disasters engaged the country's news cycles for a decade.

I was constantly troubled by the collision of complex ideas and what I saw as the technologists' Achilles heel: a total lack of reflection regarding systems-level change and unintended consequences. I had seen this first, in college, with offensive military technology, then with complex systems from automobile to financial transaction systems, to my own museum robot missteps. We follow the same model so very frequently: invent a complex system that barely works; oversell its capabilities; then blithely fail to evaluate the societal impact of that technology.

My laboratory at Carnegie Mellon, CREATE Lab, was our attempt to fight this techno-optimistic tack with a counter-narrative by explicitly orienting scientific research with community needs and values. Every project CREATE adopts is chartered through a process of engagement with community members who want lasting social change in some way that our technical innovation chops could actually support. This means years-long relationships with communities, from kindergarten teachers to neighborhood air quality advocates to climate change storytellers. In each case, the question we ask is how our inventions could empower individuals and groups to enact the positive, social changes they desire.

In Pre-K and Kindergarten classes, our educator friends were disturbed by parents' lack of engagement with what goes on in the classroom. We invented an ever-evolving system, Message from Me, that consisted of teacher training, photography technology, and a communication network that empowers the youngest children to boast about their days' activities in time for fruitful dinner conversations at home. We did years of fine-tuning, evaluation, observation—trying to ensure that the system adds to the educational experience, provides a sense of agency and power to small children, and establishes effective communication lines between parents and children.

In a project like this, I would literally shed tears when some of the success stories were captured eloquently; one mother told us how the father of their daughter had a mostly physical relationship for years—they would just wrestle, and that's it. As a year of messages arrived on the father's phone from his daughter, he began to crack open, asking her about their field trip that day, or the volcano they made with baking soda in the classroom. By the end of the year, the mother told us that father and daughter were having long, loving conversations that made her so very happy—it was a shift in emotion, expression, and love that she never dared to imagine.

The small stories like this—they made our CREATE Lab feel right to me; and yet funding was, and is, a never-ending, pitched battle. Foundations demand scale—they want projects to have large impact and be eventually national. They want to divide the dollars they give by the people served and have a denominator so huge that the project is "cheap" per person. Yet our work—the work of engaging for years with small networks of people—is the very opposite of all this. It takes time, it takes small scale, and it succeeds in the local. As with many good things in life, if you scale it up, you ruin it; what St. Louis needs and what New Orleans needs in terms of early-childhood pre-K technology will be as different as the demographics, cultures, and histories of each place.

One of our CREATE Lab projects did in fact turn out to have a scalable, national audience, and that voyage took me right back into the belly of the United States entrepreneurial system. That story begins with the challenge Pittsburgh has faced for literally more than a century: air pollution. In the early twentieth century, my adopted city was famously a "two-collar town," where anyone with a collared shirt needed to change collars midday because the level of soot dirtied anything you wore in a matter of hours.

Over the years, most of the steel plants within the city limits closed, and the business and municipal leaders began to tout Pittsburgh's quality of life, saying that our air was much cleaner than it used to be. For communities still suffering from record high asthma rates around our city, this mantra was insulting. We still had the second-worst air quality in the United States, with more than half the days of the year exceeding EPA standards. I became aware of this tension between Pittsburgh's public image and the environmental injustice of modern-day Pittsburgh as we worked more and more closely with local neighborhood organizations dedicated to advocating for the air quality that was their human right.

One such neighborhood organization was ACCAN—Allegheny County Clean Air Now. They were focused tightly on the pollution emitted by Shenango Coke Works—a massive plant on the Ohio River that reduced coal to coke, for steelmaking, twenty-four hours a day, within smelling range of more than seventy thousand residents of Ben Avon, Avalon, and other dense Pittsburgh suburbs.

We began meeting with residents and with ACCAN members regularly—in their local church meeting room on a weekly basis—for months and then years, understanding their lived experiences and their strategies for forcing change. They could tell, just looking at the plant, that illegal emissions were regularly distributing plumes of toxins into the air that flowed right over their neighborhoods. They were sweeping soot out of their porches every morning, because the accumulation was that fast. They were unable to open windows during the hot, humid summer nights, because the rotten egg smells would invade their bedrooms.

Their efforts to report their living conditions to the local health department and to the national EPA were wholly unsatisfying. The health department said, "Well, there is a paint factory and also the Shenango factory on Neville Island. We cannot tell which one is causing your stinky air; therefore, we cannot regulate either one." The factory continued emitting illegally, and simply paid fines as needed—a perfect demonstration of the concept of "pay to play." The fines were far less expensive than the repairs that were sorely needed to reduce emissions to legal, humane levels.

Listening intently to the community, we began to see how air pollution was having powerful effects on them. Asthma rates were high, and so school absences were frequent for local students. Absenteeism meant that good grades and good learning were harder to achieve, and so the local college scholarships that demanded high attendance rates were unavailable to the children. Families who considered just escaping by moving out of the area discovered that their house valuations were low because of the air toxins and the smell. Families were trapped, with poor health and all the consequences that come with these conditions, all in an area with lower-middle and middle-class incomes and little privilege to flex at lawmakers and health officials.

What's worse, as with every story that pits community against industry, we could also see a massive disparity of power. The community had voices and stories, and industry hired expert scientists with PhDs, who served up charts, data, and high-tech visuals to show that community members' claims *might* be wrong. The health department even got involved, saying that the real culprit was smoking—and that if residents would just stop smoking, everything would be much better. This is the very definition of marginalization in the face of environmental injustice, and we could see it playing out daily in our adopted community.

The project on which ACCAN and CREATE collaborated, in this context, set up a new sort of ambition. Let's empower the community to be the owners of data and information that is so high-quality, so visually convincing, that it overcomes the doubts of the health department and blows apart the false expertise of the corporate scientific consultants. Let's level the field in terms of technological fluency, then hit a home run with the true narratives of neighborhood residents.

Together, we invented and installed a camera system that videotaped and identified *every* illegal emission from Shenango, day and night, for months. We created air pollution sensors that ACCAN members installed in the attics of homes across the region, and we stacked that information together with wind direction data from federal weather sensors and even with smell reports by residents, using an app that we distributed to smart phones so people could report just how bad the air smelled: Smell Pittsburgh.

In the end, with data collection of every kind running for a year, we had an interactive website that the community could use to show visual evidence of Shenango's smoke plumes, plus the consequences: local asthma numbers, air quality readings, wind direction data.

With all this data in hand, the community invited the regional EPA director to visit a town meeting and seated him in front of a giant projection screen showing thousands of illegal emissions videos, filmed from ACCAN houses using our AI-based video system. We watched proudly from the back of the room as the residents used the website to show undeniable evidence from emissions to pollution and personal harm, and we watched family after family rise and tell the story of how air pollution was destroying their quality of life on a daily basis.

The magical moment arrived when, faced with a screenful of thousands of videos of illegal plumes, the EPA director rose to his feet, turned around, visibly upset, and said, "This is not acceptable."

This is the story of community empowerment—of rebalancing the broken power structures in our society that provide privilege, expertise, and believability to corporations and governments over the people. It is totally unacceptable that rebalancing such inequity requires years of work and foundation funding for a technology lab in a university; but that is the fight we choose to embrace.

In the end, the Shenango factory closed. The same health department that was so noncommittal earlier did a study on the effects of closing Shenango, and proudly published that asthma rates and cardiovascular disease in this community of seventy thousand residents dropped by 40 percent—just in the one year after Shenango closed. More studies recently have shown that pediatric asthma cases have fallen by a factor of five times since the closure of Shenango.

An astute reader will also ask about the elephant in the room: what about jobs? Closing that plant forced some forty local residents to lose their jobs—their livelihoods, their means of ensuring quality of life for their families. Those workers participated in the town halls. They came to the meetings, defending the corporation and pointing out the economic good that their jobs did. And they were very right to do so.

There is no simple good and bad in a story such as this. The workers lost their jobs. If the company had cleaned up their processes, spending real money on the machinery of the coke factory, a different outcome would have been possible. But in our world of profits and economic balance, the holding company found it more profitable to close the plant than to perform the needed repairs.

Yes, the CREATE Lab had a hand in the negative economic ramifications also—if we don't recognize that, we aren't being clear-eyed about the compromises and costs of what we do. Yet the experience and the result—40 percent reductions in disease for a community of seventy thousand—is something that I treasure.

The story of Shenango is one snapshot of a much bigger, national issue that does not get nearly enough airtime: poor air quality. There are some reasons why air quality, even with its massive impact on our lives, remains an elusive topic of conversation. First of all, you have the fact that a large proportion of the harm individuals face because of air quality, from COPD to childhood and adult asthma, cardiovascular disease, and even low-birthweight deliveries, derives from corporate emissions. Health departments have an easier time blaming individuals and waving off the need for national industrial cleanup, so for decades, we have heard the rhetorical flourish from local health departments: "If people would just smoke less, there would be far fewer unhealthy particles in the air that their children breathe." Never mind that smokers and non-smokers alike are exposed to toxins because of industry; it is easier for a health department to ask its residents to take personal responsibility, than to fight a battle with corporate Goliaths.

The second challenge with air pollution is that even though it kills, it has massive, sub-lethal, highly disruptive effects on tens of millions of Americans. Wars on cancer and wars on opioids can point directly to death statistics, and they can characterize the enemy as all-bad. Industrial emissions are more nuanced—after all, every corporation makes decisions about just how much money to save, and just how polluting their emissions can acceptably be. And they also decide what to do economically, balancing fines, actual repair costs, possible lawsuit costs, public relations value—and use some sort of internal calculus to create their own corporate strategy.

Then there is the problem of power imbalance. In the case of air pollution, our biggest offenders have massive power in society: economic, legal, political. The biggest harms are inflicted upon low-income neighborhoods that are dispersed throughout the country—with individual voters who have little economic power, no million-dollar lawyers, and much more limited political presence.

In the face of these incredible headwinds against real progress on air quality in the United States, we choose to invent tools at CREATE that tip the scales of power back in the direction of individual Americans—inspired by the success and promise of the Shenango experience.

One such project deserves mention because of how, as if we were playing some pathological video game, no matter how we worked to find a path forward that would empower people, new barriers rose up from the ground to block our progress. Whack-a-mole.

It all started with the recognition that, in rural communities near hydraulic fracking sites, farmers were being subjected to unknown amounts of pollution in their homes with no way to tell just how bad the air had become and, therefore, no way to even triage their day-to-day exposures. We worked to develop a low-cost air quality monitor that would show the level of particulate pollution in the home, using low-cost dust sensors and fancy computer code to turn a cheap sensor into a higher-quality, usable air quality monitor. We made a few dozen devices, conducted a pilot in Pittsburgh

and its surroundings, and were astounded by the level of empowerment that volunteers felt after living with the sensor for a month.

Using a Facebook page to stay in touch with one another, these
pioneers figured out when to crack a window open when they were
cooking; they discovered a duct-cleaning company that actually made
their forced-air systems cleaner, as opposed to other cleaning companies that just made it worse.

One volunteer discovered that the fuel oil heater was venting into
his child's bedroom due to poor exhaust placement. A rural couple was
able to tell when the pollution was blowing in from a local fracking
site and would drive to the shopping mall for the day, feeling far better with fewer asthma attacks. The stories were magical because they
showed that even a simple sensor, if it can transform the invisible into
something that can be measured, can empower individual homeowners to establish their own strategies to manage bad air.

Motivated by *Horton Hears a Who*, we named the device Speck,
created a small company to build Specks right in Pittsburgh, and went
off to Austin, Texas to unveil the product at the *South by Southwest* fes-
tival. The public release was a success, with hundreds of orders streaming in for the two-hundred-dollar device. We were on top of our game
when we discovered the first new structural roadblock we would encounter: PayPal.

We were using PayPal to take orders, and the way that PayPal oper-
ates is that the purchasers' funds flow to PayPal, then PayPal transfers
them to the business—in our case, so we can order parts and build
Speck air quality monitors. But PayPal wants to protect consumers—
so here we are, a brand-new company, receiving hundreds of thousands
of dollars in product payments. Their solution: keep the money at Pay-
Pal, because who's to say we are actually going to deliver the product?

The messaging was like something from the dystopian movie, *Brazil*. First, we received an automated message from PayPal that they
would be withholding some fraction of payment from us because they
considered us high-risk. We tried explaining to them, using a web

form, that we needed the money to purchase parts and build the Specks, precisely so we could deliver them, but that argument fell on deaf ears.

PayPal's automated system promised us they would do a two-week review and decide what fraction of the customer payments they would be withholding from us. We did our best to start building a few Specks, anxiously waiting for payment from PayPal so we could order parts. And so, after two weeks, we received our decision:

"After careful evaluation, we at PayPal have decided on the fraction of customer payments that we will withhold from Airviz, Inc. That fraction is: 100 percent."

No, really—PayPal can choose to withhold every dollar paid to them, because what if the business owner does not actually build the product? And they can do this even when the owner needs the money precisely so that they can buy parts and pay labor and build a product!

I decided to go all-in at this point, fighting a system that was clearly designed to disempower small business owners. I tried emailing and calling PayPal and could get nothing back but form emails with FAQ lists. A magical day finally arrived when I went through a friend, scored a phone number for an actual human being at PayPal, and my director of operations and I called them on speakerphone and explained the situation. She was a friendly call center agent who never steered away from the messages they had already sent us, so the call was more a review of existing emails than the delivery of any new information. So, exasperated, I asked a series of new questions.

"All these emails I am sending asking for a review of this 100 percent withholding decision—who reads these emails I send?"

"Sir, those are sent to an automated system that responds."

"Okay, but then when I disagree with the response, how do I escalate to a manager to read my complaint?"

"Sir, the management is an automated system."

"Wait, the management is automated? But at some point, can I get a human being to read my emails? The automated management system has a human supervisor. Right?"

"Those emails are only read by an automated system."

"There is no human being I can ever escalate to? Ever?"

"No, the system is automated."

This is the remarkable, real-life equivalent of an absurd video-game dead end. It seems that in the early 2000s at least, PayPal had turned over small-business relationships to AI. And we didn't even have ChatGPT yet to spin us convincing fictional stories.

I began searching news stories on-line, only to discover that what had happened to us was not at all unique—the corners of many news outlets featured stories about exactly this form of financial "hostaging" in the new world of digital sales.

And this is where I exercised a privilege that is entirely unavailable to most victims of this business crime: I had a login back then on the Huffington Post and would regularly write columns for them. I wrote a column about the total insanity of this situation, soup to nuts, and the Huffington Post published it. Within twelve hours, PayPal transferred *all* our funds to our bank account, without so much as an automated notification.

That I had to resort to privilege to have any chance at justice is—well, I want to say it's disheartening; but the problem with saying that is that, look around—it is the reality we all live, day in and day out. That is not just disheartening, that trivializes things. It is structural, and fighting against this level of injustice, broadly, ought to be a life-long effort for the whole population.

The Speck experience moved forward and, while the company never became a national brand, there are so many ways in which privilege and power negotiations cropped up time and again in the experience of trying to build an air quality monitor for the people.

Even just funding the company was an educational experience. To find the millions of dollars needed to get Airviz, Inc. off the ground,

I began flying regularly to the Bay Area, visiting both standalone venture capital firms and also investment arms of major corporate titans—the folks making chips, cellphones, and home devices that we all have.

It should come as no surprise that corporate funders did not care about the technology, nor about the story of personal empowerment that flowed from the household use of a sensor. What they cared about was just one thing: who owns all the data?

"How much information can you collect and keep on household behavior?"

"Can you collect and store information on health conditions and exercise habits?"

"Can you collect demographic information on families?"

The value that investors saw in the product was not in the physicality of a device that people will find useful, but in its ability to become an insertion point for collecting information about people and their behavior in households all over the U.S., digesting, analyzing, selling and reselling it for marketing. We were living in an age when customer information was the scarce resource, and the dollar signs they saw derived from the ability to own and digest all that data.

So, you can imagine their expressions when I would explain that we believed homeowners had the right to own their data—that we would own nothing, but rather empower them to make sense of their data for their own health strategies. This would be like Nest saying that we will give you a thermostat, but we will not collect data on how many hours a day you are home, how long your vacations are, etc. (Yeah, no, they don't say that.)

In one case, one of the very biggest VC firms in the world, Kleiner-Perkins, took a shine to our technology but was definitely underwhelmed by our story of local empowerment. But they asked for a Speck device to try out—and I left them one.

The next week, I received an email from a Kleiner contractor in China (no, really) asking how to use the device, since it was sitting on his desk now. And then, over the next month and a half, he asked ever more detailed questions about just how it worked. In China. You don't suppose they were reverse engineering the product, do you?

The best "no" that I received, however, was even more impressive than the hijacked-to-China Speck. One VC firm we visited had a beautifully appointed floor in a nondescript office building in downtown Palo Alto (this is something of a trend, actually). When we visited, we were ushered to a boardroom where my old, cheap Mac somehow magically showed our slides, wirelessly, on their state-of-the-art screen—imagine my surprise as a computer scientist when hidden features are unearthed on my own laptop.

We went through the presentation, and even stressed that we would build the devices in Pittsburgh to create local jobs and local economic impact. Every homeowner would own their own information so they can best decide how to use air pollution historical trends to find patterns for better quality of life.

The room was full of young, confident VCs, and the leader of the pack stopped me at this point. "Illah," he said, "shit runs downhill." I had never heard this phrase in my life, and here is how he explained himself.

"You're saying you are gonna make an actual device. But if you make a device, then you sell it through Amazon or Home Depot. They will force you to sell it below cost, and you have to do what they say. And if you mass-produce it in China and order ten thousand of them, the Chinese factory will make a hundred thousand, send ten thousand to you, and sell the other ninety thousand way below your cost. And if you sell it on Amazon and it does well, then Amazon will build one that's half the price and twice as good and undercut you completely. Building hardware is stupid, because shit runs downhill. Never build anything."

He walked us out a few minutes later, but he lingered in their reception lobby. He bent down and picked up a beautiful brown box that was folded like origami. "Here," he said, "take this. We have a special operation, where we have single-source cocoa from Ecuador, and we have a small company that makes us these boxes of truffles. They're awesome. They're handmade, you are going to love them. Take two. They're the absolute best."

─────────────

So, how did we find funding, after all, to get the millions of dollars that production would require? Privilege, again. I was a speaker at the World Economic Forum meeting in Davos, Switzerland—because they love to have professors there professing about trends and futures.

After a reception, I was headed back to the main conference venue when the CEO of a Fortune 100 company noticed me waiting for the free shuttle service. I knew him from college days, and he was a wonderfully friendly, engaging person.

He invited me to ride with him in his limousine and I accepted. In the car, I mentioned the company and our mission, and the money flowed. That's it—privilege upon privilege upon a chance encounter—a whole scaffolding of opportunity, from days together at Stanford, to a professorship at an elite school, to an invitation to Davos, to an invitation into the limousine where it happens.

One final story from the Airviz days merits telling. When we began selling Speck air quality monitors, we also started receiving hundreds of emails from communities that could not afford to buy a two-hundred-dollar device but were desperate to begin documenting how local industry was polluting their air. So, we had a nice idea: make it a library book!

Libraries are already logistically set up to lend and receive physical books, and they are on the prowl for all the services that make them relevant to the twenty-first century. Why not electronic devices that are founts of information but are too expensive for many in low-income communities to purchase?

We did it, in Pittsburgh at first and then nationally, across two dozen libraries, for several years. We gave the Specks to libraries for free, since they, too, cannot afford it with their tight budgets; and then we worked to create literature that helped homeowners borrow them and establish a sense of what to do in their homes, instead of just crossing into a state of pollution-anxiety.

Through this library program, one of the biggest health insurance corporations in the U.S. became aware of us and set up a meeting. I traveled to their headquarters, to the top floor, to meet their researchers and their Chief Technology Officer. The meeting went well as I explained what the device does and told stories of personal empowerment from our customers. My pitch to them was direct: let's put these in their customers' homes, and help their customers learn to improve their own air quality in the home.

I bet, if we can save even one emergency room visit a year for each customer with asthma or COPD, we will more than compensate for the cost of the Specks. So then, let's have you, a giant insurance company, pay for the device and put it in your clients' homes—it's both a financial win for the insurance company, and a health win for your clients.

Their response was enthusiastic, with a twist. Let's do the experiment, they said. But we have one request. "Make the screen blank." I was confused—my model of the test was to show homeowners how bad their air is and help them see that they can take actions to ameliorate it. A blank screen gives them zero information. "Exactly what we want," they said.

"We want to know how polluted it is in their homes, but we don't want them to change behavior because that would ruin the experiment."

Yes, that's how science works. I get it. And this puts a fine point on the extreme injustice of "the way science works." This is not a vaccine, it's literally a self-empowerment tool. To collect data with it, and not even provide the benefit it's designed to provide—that, to me, is lower than low.

If you pull back, from industry to health agencies to PayPal to venture capitalists to health insurance, the message is really all the same.

The incentive structures and payoff systems we have in our society are not only unaligned with social good; they are actually maligned against social justice.

This is the truth of the world we inhabit; our best money and brains pour fuel on an innovation system that is, nationally, entirely at odds with the prospect of equity, fairness, and justice. Shit runs downhill only because we make it so.

Chapter 15

Immigrant Death

I have completed my sixth decade of life, and every new decade has layered my memories with the births and deaths of those whom I love. Yet there is a unique mark left on me by the most intimate birth and most intimate death that I witnessed over all those years. Personally witnessing the transition from life to death is rare for me—I am not a physician, and for many good reasons, we are all shielded from the moment of death, instead reinforcing our love and memories through rituals among our families and friends.

But birth is different. As a father, I had the privilege to observe the first moments of my eldest daughter. The hospital was in San Francisco, 2004, and I remember her face exactly as she emerged into our world. Her eyes were open and silver-colored; her mouth was closed and motionless. Her whole face looked like a statue, eyes open, and then an instant later two things happened in unison: her eyes closed and her mouth opened as everything about her animated, arms waving to her first cry. At the time, I was struck by that transition, and over the next months, looking at my newborn's silver-colored, young eyes staring back at me, I thought frequently of that moment, that transition from stillness to life.

A few years later, my paternal grandmother entered hospice care, and I saw her death with the same intimacy. My grandmother had a unique story of immigration. She moved from Iran directly to Fayetteville, Arkansas, with her husband and her youngest daughter, who lived with her and cared for her. She was a school principal and owner in Teheran, and the transition from work in Iran was directly to a retired life in Fayetteville, a town with strong evangelical Christian roots and heavy southern accents.

As with many immigrant families, where one pioneer goes many follow, so a small nucleus of Nourbakhshes had set up shop in the heart of the American South. Talking with them was a trip, because we would switch between standard Farsi in the accent of Teherani inhabitants, and deeply accented Southern English.

What's more, the evangelical community of Fayetteville provided support and a sense of belonging to my aunt, so I also code-switched from the Muslim family of my immediate Kansas City Nourbakhshes to the born-again Christians of my southern family. We would have Persian kabobs for lunch, grilled outside in the old ways with steamed Basmati rice, then go thrifting and antiquing in the best traditions of the South. My grandmother and grandfather did not convert, but they were surrounded by generous Christianity, and the support network of their caregivers were all, in turn, very religious. So I saw Christmas trees and Nowruz celebrations; singing and music-playing with a Persian hammered dulcimer; then off to church for the younger, born-again contingent of our family.

Hospice arrived for my grandmother after great hardship over decades—a common story for all who live to an old age and experience traumatic injury. I was there, visiting her in hospital, then accompanying her into a hospice facility that was just beautiful: caring, gentle, and full of the empathy we would each wish for our loved ones.

I was far from alone: there were all my northern family members, from Boston and points west, and my southern family members, my Fayetteville aunt and cousins. In addition, my aunt had regular companionship at the hospice from her church support network, staying nonstop just like us. My grandmother was in a private room with a half-dozen chairs, mostly occupied by a two-religion, three-country support network. The Christian delegation would murmur quiet prayers regularly, and the Iranian immigrants from the north would stand silent, pace, and worry.

Hospice is an emotionally taxing, one-way process. The nurses help greatly by talking us through the changes we should expect, and in mentoring us so that we could provide comfort to my grandmother in every possible way. Providing that comfort is a ritual that, I'm sure, is more for our sake, but we spent days dabbing sponges on her lips to keep them from chapping; making sure she was just the right temperature by moving blankets about; moving pillows to find comfortable postures for her head.

But hospice is unknowable along one special consideration: nobody, no matter what they tell you, knows how much longer the patient will live. We wait, we comfort, for days; and we observe two cultures—the Iranian and the Arkansan—providing care and comfort in distinct ways around the margins of one-another.

The unknowability of the time of death puts a toll on the working person's plans; and so a milling naturally happens after a few days, with family coming and going, checking in and then leaving to do chores from home and work before returning for another check-in several hours or days later. The process of acknowledging dying becomes strangely woven into daily routines.

It was after several days, with milling becoming the norm for how we each danced around the space and our own obligations, that a confluence of circumstances changed everything for me. My brother flew back home to deal with patients, convinced that my grandmother was still long for this world. My uncle left on an errand in town. My aunt went to fetch something from her home, fifteen minutes away. My aunt's friend from church, who was praying in the corner, stood up and walked out of the room.

For the first time, I found myself alone with my grandmother after all these days in hospital and hospice. She was laboring to breathe, her eyes closed for days now, and her mouth open. I moved my chair from the doorway by the curtain to reposition myself right alongside her left arm, by her face.

I had wanted, for days, to give her something familiar from home—something she had perhaps not listened to during the duress of this final illness. I had heard and appreciated the prayers spoken by our Christian friends and family; but my grandmother was born of a time and place where her prayers were the prayers of Islam, in the language of Arabic, not English.

There is a particular standard prayer that Muslims perform in the morning; it has two repeated sections, two chapters, and is performed in Arabic, regardless of the mother language of the Muslim. I held my grandmother's left hand with both of my hands, then recited this two-part prayer, which takes just a few minutes, out loud into the silence surrounding me.

There is a final line in this prayer—a stanza in which we say *Salaam*, or peace, with three variations of wording. The third and final time, we say: "Peace go with you and the mercy and blessings of God." That is the very final line of the entire morning prayer.

I was watching her face, holding her hand, finishing this poem that I had wanted to recite for days, but felt strange about performing in front of people who may consider it insulting, or challenging, or just out of place.

Her eyes had been closed, her mouth open, for days. I finished saying *"Assalamu-alaikum wa Rahmatullahe wa Barakaatuh"* and stopped, finished. After just two beats, my grandmother's eyes opened, her mouth closed, and she stopped breathing.

I was instantly reminded, in that moment, of my daughter's face as she was born. I saw the same expression—eyes open, mouth closed, zero movement. It was shocking, actually. I felt I was witnessing a duality that I would never be able to fully comprehend.

Did my Muslim prayer give my grandmother peace? Did she connect a tendril of her past comforts to the present moment as she heard my words? I would like to think so. I would like to think that, in the middle of Fayetteville, Arkansas, what my grandmother needed in order to let go was a reflection of her youth in Iran—of the culture and traditions that permeated her origins.

We are immigrants. We are who we are because of the relationships we have built here, in America. My grandmother was Arkansan, a naturalized U.S. citizen, for decades. She had wonderful support structures in Fayetteville, including an entire born-again community that cared for her, transitively, through her youngest daughter. But that is not all of her identity.

We do not transition. We grow. My grandmother was forever a school principal from Teheran. A Muslim-Iranian. Her old ways were also part of her, and I was anxious to provide a connection to those ways even though it was awkward in a new world.

What we do for the dying is also for our own benefit—for our own sanity. That is always true. But I do believe there is an elemental need we have, in death, to also connect to the ways of our birth, no matter how distant that place and culture may have become.

Chapter 16

Two Left Turns

I have been teaching Ethics and Robotics since 1996. The discussions that the students and I have, in the round, provide me with yearly insights on the anxieties and concerns that students have about how their computer science and robotics degrees will translate into careers, what kind of impact they hope to have on the world around them, and how they think about the features of a successful and rewarding life.

Over twenty-five years, I have seen themes that grow and wane in their eyes, often swinging right back into focus ten years later, like fashion. Technologies for war; surveillance and invasions of privacy; massive wealth derived from entrepreneurial tech companies—these are topics that are essential to the students some years, and entirely missing from their attention other years.

The urgency of these themes stems from what's happening in the greater world around us: 9/11, Google's explosive success, Facebook's Metaverse, Cambridge Analytica, drone war in the Middle East, Enron, ChatGPT, the big financial meltdown. The students always hold current events, their computer skills, and major social themes in a sort of three-way balance, and they wonder how to decide just what to do about a future that seems, at times, bleak.

In class, we use current events, and the students' own questions, to probe how they think about their own responsibility as engineers who will help to guide the future. They dig into the question of culpability: is it all right for a junior programmer to join a company and create new technology on spec, or is there a further responsibility that the engineer has to the downstream use that will inevitably result from that new innovation?

I introduce multiple ethical frameworks to the students, from the character ethics espoused by Aristotle to consequentialism, where you weigh the good and bad effects of your decision as if the scales of ethics are mathematically fine-tuned. The students practice using various ethical frameworks to weigh possible technology projects, both historical and imagined.

We discuss how there is no one right analysis in such a messy, social space; but that, by developing their own personal grammar of ethics, each student can fluently consider their own personal choices rather than stepping forward into opportunities oblivious to *why* they are choosing one path over other alternatives.

Even as topics like privacy and warfighting come and go in terms of student interest, there has always been one line of questioning that students ask about, without fail—either in class or in one-on-one appointments with me during office hours. They come in and sit down. "I have this opportunity that I am considering for summer internship and then probably full-time work. I am uncomfortable with the work, but it pays well. And if I don't do it, someone else will. So ... can I justify doing it?"

"If I don't do it, someone else will" is where so many students begin, and the way I respond hearkens back to my own graduate school encounter with autonomous tank control. Because, yes, someone else will do anything you find unpalatable. And you are busy getting a degree in Computer Science or Electrical Engineering, so you are, by definition, a creator, a maker of new inventions. You are not a social scientist or ethicist, and you may have very little experience with political advocacy. So, what choice do you have?

Could you decide that, actually, instead of building that system, you are going to become a policy expert and advocate for system-level change so that no one needs to build that system? That is a stretch for most. And such a departure from engineering is probably not going to pay off your college debt.

But this binary choice between doing the well-paying engineering job or making very little money and squandering your talent is a fiction, because these are never the only two possible paths. There are multitudes of skill-matched projects you can do that you are implicitly choosing not to do when you take that unpalatable job because if you don't do it, someone else will.

The question is, have you thought actively about everything you *want* to do, everything you're *talented* for doing—and are you alright actively deciding *not* to do all those things, just so you can do a job that is uninspiring?

The conversation shifts with the student, from how to say no to a superficially good career, to how to imaginatively consider a set of careers that are both exciting and inspiring. An economics-based way to think about this mindset shift is to value the potential for regret. How much regret will you have if you just take that job at Google, incrementally improving the amount of ad profits they bring home, when you consider what you could do with the next ten years? How costly is that regret? How much do you value all the things you say no to, when you take that job and become a big player in a complex coding machine where the business rules and the values of the company are beyond the reach of your authority?

My very personal connection to this line of thinking stretches even further back, to high school—literature class, where my Scottish teacher had us read Walker Percy's *The Second Coming*. That book upended my view of suicide, and with that shift, my value system regarding any choice we make that closes out the possibility of actively doing anything in the world.

In Percy's book I believe the protagonist's experiment with suicide stopped, not just because of the horrible toothache he developed as he waited for a miracle in a cave, but because he fell into a deeper realization brought on by physical pain: if I choose suicide, then I cancel out the possibility of doing and feeling anything else.

My personal version of this logic lifted me away from suicide, specifically, any time I settle for an uncomfortable path: "There are no passive actions." Every time I choose to act, I want to be sure I have actively decided that I know the alternatives and that they really are less good—that I am making the right decision on balance. Otherwise, I believe I pay an unacknowledged price; that, to me, is unacceptable during a short life.

My students receive a gentler version of this logic, along with examples from various ethics frameworks, as I hope to instill in them the sensibility that they can take the time, every season, to actively consider their choices, and to recognize the alternatives they have chosen to avoid just as explicitly as the path they have chosen to inhabit.

Once I was at Carnegie Mellon and starting up a lab, I wanted the entire lab group to have this same habit of explicit reflection about the lab's direction—a sort of system-wide version of the same existential thinking that my students face. Each time I lead a research group along such an exercise, I become giddy at the prospect that someone in the research group might think of a direction we have not considered yet—a direction that can be life-changing to our group as a whole, and bold in how we achieve a new level of public good. I have always called these opportunities "left turns," and two of them stand out across all these decades.

My first left turn happened at NASA/Ames in Moffett Field, California, in 2003. I was sitting at a table, leading the Intelligent Robotics Group at NASA as a tenured civil servant, and I asked a question that we wrestled with for a full month.

"If we had infinite resources in this group, what would we do with our time together?"

How I got to ask this question at NASA, of all places, is a story of the final application of my Futureproofing Formula because of the biggest anxiety every professor faces in their career: tenure.

For the uninitiated: the tenure vote is the ultimate judgement day for professors. It can only have two possible outcomes, and the decision itself is unavoidable. When I was hired, the tenure do-or-die decision would be nine years after my hire date. One year before the deadline, the university sends requests for reference letters to more than a dozen senior researchers in the field, asking them to rate me compared to my peers.

Has this person made a contribution significant enough for tenure—which often is posed in terms of field-building; has this person made a seminal contribution that defines a new sort of field of research, or a new kind of solution that many now appreciate? The bar is so high it is intimidating, for nine years. And when the faculty eventually vote, a no vote means they give you six months' notice, and you must find a new job outside the university. A "yes" vote means they will never make a decision about you staying or going again—you have a permanent job until you retire.

My problem going into the tenure year was two-fold. First, I had never forgotten the threat made against me, specifically for my tenure case, by the colleague who didn't want me to take on my very first museum robot project. And second, the work I had been doing in robotics was spectacularly unconventional at a time when unconventional was not nearly as common as it is today.

I was working on educational robots, specifically for middle school girls. I was working on navigation for electric wheelchairs for quadriplegic users. I was researching and teaching ethics, and on the dangers of robotic technologies in warfare. I had already heard, through the faculty grapevine, that my tenure case would be touch-and-go, so I had pretty solid evidence that this whole career path may well go south.

So, I did the futureproofing maneuver yet again. I contacted my colleagues at NASA/Ames, because I knew that Mars Exploration Rovers were on their way, flying between the planets, and the spotlight on NASA was bright and exciting. NASA made me a permanent job offer: a tenured civil service position as the director of the Intelligent Robotics Group at NASA/Ames, which was near Mountain View, California and therefore a short drive from my mother, to boot. I took the job and went on leave from Carnegie Mellon—a perfectly legal maneuver that is also entirely insane, because who leaves *before* getting denied tenure, but still expects the university to consider their tenure case?

I moved my house and family to San Francisco—Bernal Heights—and so I fully invested in this new, alternative future. Just like my special formula: invent a future that you would actually love, embrace it, and make the jump. Then, if the judgement you hate goes awry, no worries. If the judgement goes well, you have unexpected good news.

Before moving, I read a library of books to prepare for this transition—two books on orbital mechanics so I could speak intelligently about spacecraft trajectories; and three books on the history of NASA and the history of its directors; and one more book on leadership, since the Intelligent Robotics Group would be easily ten times larger than any group I had led before, not to mention multiples larger in terms of annual spending.

I restyled my commute from bicycling in Pittsburgh to the reality of Bay Area traffic: ride a Yamaha Virago from home to the Caltrain station, ride the Caltrain to Mountain View, then use a kick scooter to kick from the Caltrain station to NASA's main gate. I even reinvented my work week, explaining to all my new colleagues that I work from home on Fridays. That line worked, and I found myself enjoying sunny San Francisco and working from cafés every Friday, decades before COVID and well before our new four-day work week gained traction.

The high point of my NASA experience was, of course, the interaction with all the space researchers. The IRG staff came from across a broad age range, with skills in computer science, Artificial Intelligence, mechanics and electronics, computer vision—everything that makes an engineer feel like they are in a Disneyland of talent. And they were kind, excited and happy to band together for new projects and ideas.

What's more, my supervisory position gave me the chance to flash my NASA civil service badge and access other facilities: Johnson Space Center, JPL, and NASA Headquarters in Washington, DC.

We worked, with CREATE, on an educational robot that museums could use to help visitors understand how the Mars Exploration Rovers work, and as part of outreach training, I got to travel to Texas and meet with the astronaut corps—all the astronauts—to train them on how to demonstrate our educational rovers to children. They were the most engaged, the sharpest people I had ever sat with, and that made yet another powerful impression on me regarding our space program—remember that the space shuttle would be functioning still for seven more years when I was at NASA. It is no exaggeration to say that, sitting with the astronauts, I felt dumber than I have ever felt in a group—before or since.

When the Mars Exploration Rovers landed in January 2004, NASA entered a period of intense work and also constant jubilation. The rovers were controlled directly by teams at JPL in Pasadena, and our IRG researchers were responsible for processing and displaying the panoramic imagery that each rover was shooting on Mars.

The panoramic cameras on these rovers were a new innovation. Using a set of high-quality cameras trained on one spot in the Martian landscape, the imaging system would take a picture, then pan the camera head, rotating just a bit so the next picture would have borders overlapping just slightly with the previous picture. The resulting picture series, raw ingredients for a massive panoramic image, were sent back to Earth, where members of our IRG team stitched the images together to create a single, seamless, very high-resolution photograph from the rover's point of view.

Members of our IRG group, in Northern California, traveled to JPL to live there on shifts, managing the process of panorama creation and the presentation of these panoramic images to scientists, who spent hours studying every detail in the images. Our IRG visitors in Southern California lived on Martian "sols" rather than Earth days, so they woke and went to bed, like their JPL colleagues, synchronized with the Mars daylight hours when the rovers were in operation. Over the course of a few weeks, we watched from Northern California as they messaged us at nine in the morning, then gradually evening, then later, 4 A.M., 5 A.M., and finally right back to our morning in Earth time. It was a time of technical achievement, with the promise of new science and new discoveries on a literally daily basis.

For me, the most inspiring aspect of our work at NASA/Ames was watching the relationship that developed between the Mars scientists and the Martian image panoramas. Before Mars, I always thought of photographs in two ways: either as triggers for reminiscing about something in the past, or as an expressive and artful medium for creativity.

Watching the scientists look at high-resolution panoramas suggested an entirely new relationship between image and discovery. They studied a panorama and debated, at length, which part of this giant image deserved a zoomed-in look. Then they would ask the team to generate a higher resolution closeup of that specific, narrow part.

On and on this attentional rock-turning process would play out, with scientists studying the details of the image then interactively swimming through the image for hours, exploring details that are invisible initially, but reveal themselves as they zoom in further and further. The scientists did science with a photograph, both discerning new information about Mars, and also using all the data to make crucial decisions about just which direction *Spirit* and *Opportunity* should drive next.

For me, this was a mindset shift in the concept of photography. The photograph was neither art nor a static bookmark documenting a place and time; it was its own miniature universe that could be studied, explored actively, and could even yield new discoveries hidden in the initial, zoomed-out view.

As the Mars mission went on, breaking every endurance record, three different threads from my NASA experience wove together to create just the right conditions for that first left turn. I was in awe of how some of the astronauts described their emotional perspective about Earth changing when they viewed the whole planet from orbit. I was excited by the degree to which an interactive panorama could be the object of study, just like a rainforest or a rock outcropping. And I was reading management books about how to provide a strong sense of agency to a group of researchers.

It was in this context that, at our weekly IRG meeting at NASA/Ames, I introduced the blue-sky question for the whole group as a thought experiment.

"If we had infinite resources in this group, what would we do with our time together?"

One idea struck a chord quickly—could the ability to seamlessly view our own planet and explore it, the way scientists were exploring Mars panoramas, change the global sense of empathy that our brothers and sisters feel around the world? We joked about accomplishing this by sending all congressional delegates to orbit Earth, then did the calculations to convince ourselves that the amount of carbon we would release would make the mission entirely unethical—even if a large fraction of them came back ready to collaboratively solve our problems.

So, we started imagining near-infinite zooming panoramas. What if policymakers—and for that matter, everyone else—could see Earth as a living organism, and then zoom in and continue zooming in, as if falling, until they could make out the intimacy of a family dealing with their very local world—fishing sustainably at the edge of the Amazon, for instance. What if the entire Earth was its own giant, infinitely zoomable panorama that connected natural phenomena and animal and human life at all levels of scale?

Our hypothesis was that, with infinite resources to create something like this, we might bring people together to more meaningfully solve our joint challenges. And then the next natural step revealed itself to us: authorship. We are creatures of narrative—it is our stories that empower us to share our values and aspirations. What if, instead of a zoomable Earth that is produced and presented, ready for exploration, the interactive world was actually a collection of zoomable panoramas, miniature universes authored by everyone, everywhere—to share their realities, their celebrations, their challenges in this new medium?

All these discussions were swirling in our conversations; and this was all before Google Earth existed as a product. Maps, back then, were images you clicked on, north by northwest for instance, to awkwardly pan over to an adjacent map. Zooming was just on the edge of being born as a fluid element of digital maps. Keyhole had recently been purchased by Google and they were looking for ways to organize information using Keyhole's whole-planet views.

Today, it is remarkable how hard it is to imagine that world in which the metaphor of a map was so very different, and how low-resolution and static digital photographs were all taken by small point-and-shoot digital cameras since there were no camera lenses on cellphones yet.

The left turn—co-constructed by a number of people at NASA/Ames along with friends and colleagues across the nation—was to create the robotic mechanism that could turn everyone into an author of explorable, large-scale panoramas, and then distribute this technology so broadly that it would change the way we share globally.

Members of IRG created prototype hardware that fit on a camera tripod, held a small digital point-and-shoot camera, and moved it around a scene, using a tiny robotic finger to press the shutter button repeatedly to take hundreds of digital pictures that could then be stitched together. Fifty million, one hundred million, and eventually billions of pixels would become rendered in this way, into one single, explorable image.

But now the problem was how to share such massive images. My colleagues developed techniques for streaming just the right pixels to a computer's web browser from a central server with massive disk drives capable of storing entire mini-universes. Now a user could zoom in or seamlessly pitch the camera view up and down, left and right, and explore the information buried in the panorama. Available inside that panorama, as one explores deeper and deeper, are a multitude of new views and scenes—zoom in on a Hawaiian rainforest and you can begin to identify, in zoomed-in portions of the giant panorama, all the spiders in the forest. So, we created a second form of authorship: the user would be able to find interesting details, then generate new snapshots and publish those as well—snapshots within interactive pictures.

The metaphor of the image became, to us, the act of exploration and sharing. One person may create a new mini-universe; but thousands across the world would be able to explore it, annotate it with new snapshots, and create conversations that would span the globe and cross-cultural divides. Viewers became authors, and so we saw this new medium as a form of convivial celebration regarding our planet, from the biological and structural to the social and ritual.

Just as these prototypes were engineered and constructed, the faculty at Carnegie Mellon decided, grumpily, to go ahead with my tenure vote in spite of the fact that I had flipped the script and left *before* being rejected instead of waiting for dismissal.

I remember how I finally received the tenure vote result. I was standing in a pay phone box across the street from my Tokyo hotel, and had used a calling card to connect to the Robotics Institute's director. The line was poor, and I had to ask twice to figure out if he was giving me good news or bad news. I sprinted back to the hotel, and jumped on top of the full-size bed, where my infant daughter was peacefully laying on her back.

I jumped up and down with joy and she started getting bounced up in the air, laughing all the while. I nearly bounced her off the bed and stopped jumping. A nine-year weight had been lifted off my back. I could imagine doing the research I wanted to do without feeling like I would be kicked off my research stage at any moment. It was not an exhilarating feeling of power or agency or accomplishment—but rather a wash of relief from a never-ending sense of anxiety and fear.

With tenure in hand, I retired from NASA a few months later and returned to Carnegie Mellon, with our GigaPan panorama project. I was joined at CMU by colleagues from NASA who also transferred to CMU to push this work ahead full-time.

Over the next few years, GigaPan became a public website that hosted high-resolution panoramas where authors could share them, and viewers could snapshot and annotate regions within. The robotic hardware evolved and advanced, and we commercialized it into a publicly available kit that would transform any point-and-shoot camera, and later any digital SLR, into a panorama machine.

As GigaPan photographs took root, we managed to nearly break CMU's internet. Barack Obama was elected, and a professional photographer used our equipment to create the most popular GigaPan ever: a massive zoomable panorama of Obama's inauguration from the press box, high above the crowds and with direct line of sight to the stage and the massive audience. As thousands and then millions explored and snapshotted the inauguration GigaPan, our servers at Carnegie Mellon began using more bandwidth than all other computers at CMU combined; and the university leadership joined in the fun, zooming in on Abraham Lincoln's bible in Michelle Obama's hands, on each Supreme Court justice's expression, on the sheet music of the brass band's music stands.

Our original left turn in creating this system was focused on global empathy; and to cross that line, we developed relationships with the two best organizations that I could have wished for: National Geographic and UNESCO. National Geographic led photography camps all around the world, and we connected to extraordinary photographers and camp coordinators. UNESCO, the United Nation's education arm, connected to school municipalities internationally, and they gave us direct access to schools and schoolchildren in dozens of countries, where we could create modern versions of pen pals through interactive panoramic sharing.

We took GigaPan robots and camera equipment to countries and territories through these partnerships, teaching children how to use the equipment and create panoramas, upload them, and then share them across the world—and we left the equipment at each location freely, so they would have never-ending access. Trinidad and Tobago, Switzerland, Soweto, Cape Flats, rural Pennsylvania, Pine Ridge Reservation, Bath, Haiti—these were just some of the places that we visited together.

I learned so many lessons over those years. I learned to walk around anything I wish to photograph—all the way around—and notice how light and reflections shift from every angle. I learned to wake up before dawn, and constantly search during the golden hour. I learned that, in the lowest-income regions we visited, the thirst for new technology and the children's excitement around technical photography was just as insatiable—they would gladly skip lunch hour to geek out over the technology, author their own stories, and share them with children from other religions, customs, and countries. I learned that images— even interactive ones—are an instant way to forge common ground between cultures; our visual cortex is less bigoted, less caricaturing, than our language centers, and so we can bypass some of our failings by starting with the most moving imagery possible.

I learned to slow way down—a GigaPan panorama acquisition can take ten, twenty minutes; it's like old-fashioned photography that way. So, as the author, you stop, you tend to your tripod, and then as your robot is moving your camera for fifteen minutes, you engage in dozens of conversations with locals who start by asking you about the equipment, and then from there the conversation blossoms in every direction.

In the end, what National Geographic and UNESCO most fully taught me was that even if you wish to have global impact on, say, empathy and peace, you must focus your vision and your action at the microlocal scale. Everything good comes from the most personal, intimate, local relationships that are built patiently and slowly, and as a friend of mine says, "move at the speed of trust." How poetic that this entire attitude is almost perfectly opposite to the values espoused by Big Tech, where inventions are global and inventors are supposed to have massive impact through scale and speed, moving fast and breaking things frequently.

As the GigaPan work progressed, we also forged a relationship with a local foundation in Pittsburgh that normally funded local artists but found the artistry of our technological panoramas to be compelling. The Fine Foundation saw the potential in our work to bridge the gap between science and art, and through their grantmaking we began a new program, one that we named Fine Outreach for Science.

Beginning with the Macarthur Award recipient list, we invited world-leading scientists in every imaginable branch of science to attend annual FOFS GigaPan workshops. As Fine Fellows, we explained to them in award letters that they would come together in a cross-discipline workshop, where we would teach them how to use GigaPan equipment and send them home with their very own equipment for science documentation and public science communication.

The Fine workshops were beyond extraordinary. First of all, people we never dreamt of meeting said "yes" because they were interested in the new equipment, so we met some of our true heroes. A scientist who walked across Africa; soil biologists who are world-renowned for understanding the dangers of monoculture-based agriculture; the most prolific National Geographic photographers on the planet; ecologists, geologists, botanists, entomologists.

The workshops were magical because these individuals were usually steeped in their own siloes, meeting their disciplinary colleagues for deep dives. But now they had an excuse to be amongst curious, engaging thinkers outside their own disciplinary boundaries for three days, talking about how interactive imagery can help them document their work, inform their students, and engage with the public.

I remember teachers in geology and biodiversity describing how they used GigaPan to conduct pre-field analysis: their students would zoom through a GigaPan of a rainforest or a geologic structure in-class, before a field trip, and develop an eye for how to notice the scientific features of the place. Then, only after they had developed that visual intimacy with the place, would they pile into a bus and actually go there. The students would establish a fluid connection to place and an ability to see the science in detail that far outshone what was possible before.

Many fellows came to me and said this was the most inspiring conference that they had ever attended—there was no sense of competitiveness; instead, there was wonder and discovery at how innovation can bring totally disparate fields of inquiry together—how they all cared, deeply, for our planet and for how people rethink their relationship to place.

When they returned to the field with GigaPans in tow, the panoramas they created were remarkable. They used GigaPans in scientific papers, they shared them publicly on our website, and we printed massive-scale versions that still decorate the walls of the Computer Science college at CMU. The scientific output resulting from their work was so expressive that we began a conference series, bringing them back together for presentations of their GigaPan-documented work—and they loved the reunions.

We ran our final Fellows workshop in Estes Park, Colorado, with all the scientists going to Rocky Mountain National Park to practice their panoramic photography. The high mountain setting, combined with scientists of all stripes looking at the geologic, botanic, and animal features of the place, was a high point for me to learn to be constantly slower, more patient in places of nature—to let it wash over me and nurture an eye for what is unseen.

Foundations cannot fund the same gig forever, so we eventually finished this seven-year Fine Outreach mission. Modern technology began to catch up with us, too—soon iPhones had cameras, and before long, cellphones enabled users to create panoramas just by spinning the phone around by hand. Of course, these images do not have a billion pixels, and surprisingly, that void has never been filled in a satisfactory way. Our old archival website, GigaPan, still receives millions of visitors and hosts hundreds of new, massive panoramas every month. And I have lifelong friendships today with some of the Fine scientists.

One of the owners of Keyhole, when they were selling that global satellite visualization system to Google, told me that sometimes a spotlight will focus on a team and a project and, for a time, that work shines brightly. Then the spotlight moves on. The idea of global empathy through interactive imagery was bold and became successful, thanks to the efforts of dozens of engineers and more, from NASA to private companies to Carnegie Mellon. The spotlight did indeed pass us by several years later. But even this year, school districts in West Virginia are rediscovering the power of the interactive images in our database and are finding brand new ways to integrate these images into classroom explorations.

The second left turn I want to share was born indirectly from the lessons we learned from the consequences of GigaPan—years later. When GigaPan's funding finished for its various missions, our CREATE Lab continued to press the technology forward along new dimensions—and the very first such breakout was to explore a panoramic video through time as well as space.

Time brought nature to life, and the new technology that we developed made it possible to give users the ability to explore a mini universe of visual beauty through both space and time simultaneously. Using our own robotic equipment, we were able to capture plants growing with both fine detail in space and rapid photography over time. Playing that footage back and exploring the interactive video, like a moving GigaPan, lets botanists see circumnutating, the circular motions of plants at human-visible speed.

Before long, this technology, which we termed the Time Machine, took on a planetary challenge: can we create an explorable, moving video of the entire Earth? NASA provided us access to all Landsat satellite images of the planet, with multiple passes each month across every region of Earth. Then, Google lent us tens of thousands of computers in their server farm so we could stitch the satellite images together, finding cloudless shots for every acre of land since 1984. The result of this intense computational jigsaw puzzle was that we created a space-time-explorable, planetary archive of every change visible from space.

We called this successor to GigaPan, EarthTime. The stories we were able to tell using EarthTime were heartbreaking. We could zoom into the Amazon River basin and watch as a single road in virgin forest gave way to a small town and then, over just a few years, the complete deforestation of one of the most valuable natural assets of our world.

We could zoom into Las Vegas and watch the massive growth of the city, eating the desert around it voraciously and replacing it with green golf courses and buildings—and then we could zoom out just slightly and show Lake Mead, just next door, shrinking exactly as Las Vegas grows. We could see glaciers retreating, lakes in the Middle East disappearing because of poor water management, entire cities in China growing and filling all the rural land between cities.

The visuals were so compelling that the World Economic Forum asked us to show them, interactively, to world leaders at Davos every year so they could see what is really happening with their own eyes. I remember one year, when Jair Bolsonaro was representing Brazil, stating that there is no deforestation happening—just as I was simultaneously showing world leaders direct satellite timelapses of that very deforestation in the Brazilian state of Rondonia. Visual evidence fought a battle against empty rhetoric in real time.

The EarthTime work matured and continues to grow to this day. Thousands of layers of information stack extra data on top of Earth's video imagery, for instance showing how a protected indigenous tribe's boundaries stopped deforestation in its tracks; how drought and agricultural collapse caused massive forced migrations across country borders; and how economic inequality has spread since World War II, led by the United States—another unfortunate way in which our country is often a world leader.

But there is a fundamental challenge with EarthTime that GigaPan never suffered. GigaPan connected children to each other, across country and continent, around intimate images at the human level: spice markets, mosques, churches, festivals, local streets. It was at once intimate, local, and international. The children developed shared language, empathy, and curiosity—all habits of mind that will be valuable throughout their lives.

EarthTime, in contrast, shows world leaders the global trends that are shaping planetary change: resource extraction, massive climate upheaval, global wealth inequity, global burden of disease. They see evidence that is not intimate, but global; and they see problems that can seem intractable on human scales. So, they become anxious, and then they focus down, defensively, on the challenges they can surmount in their local municipalities.

I remember one particular day at Davos; the entire South African delegation found me, and they asked for time with the EarthTime interface in our situation room. I walked in with them, and they asked for a data layer we have on top of satellite imagery—thanks to Climate Central—that shows just how sea level rise will eradicate coastal areas, meter by meter. They asked me to zoom and pan to specific locations all around the coast of South Africa, and then to play the sea level rise visualizations on top of Landsat satellite imagery, zooming in close enough to see coastal plots disappear.

They gasped, and I asked why. We were focusing on the eradication of their personal coastal vacation homes, and they were seeing the unthinkable. We spent quality time talking about the causes of this threat and the ways in which their country could play a role in reversing the trends we were tracking—but this very effective discussion was borne out of their most personal connections. Urgency starts in the personal.

I saw the power that the local wields over the global that day, and that mentality stayed with me when I walked into the second major left turn of my career. During a visit to the President's conference room at CMU, I was asked to linger after a large meeting. Our president had a puzzle for me.

Many universities, ours included, had been courting longer-term, strategic relationships with foundations, so that the university could win uninterrupted, multi-year funding commitments that enable doing the meaningful work that pays dividends only after years of effort. In the case of one specific foundation in town, The Heinz Endowments, our university team was struggling over the question of just what they would want to fund, strategically, for years on end.

This was the blue-sky question again, but the tables were turned; I was not directing the question at my staff in NASA, I was seated on a couch and was being asked, honestly, what would be truly compelling to Heinz—no constraints? The germ of the idea flowed very quickly. I had known the Heinz program officers, the trustees, and the president of this foundation for years, and I greatly respected the values that guided their funding decisions. Their core concern centered on local equity: on the very obvious inequality of opportunity faced by residents of southwestern Pennsylvania.

I had made visualizations, thanks to their funding, examining mortgage approvals and denials, life expectancy, asthma rates among children, rent costs as a fraction of income, and commute costs in money and time. By every one of these measures, our region divided people, by geography, income, and skin color, into winners and losers so starkly that it was breathtaking.

The problems are not just independent, either. If you pull on the thread of air pollution in Pittsburgh, for instance, air currents concentrate the toxic chemicals in specific neighborhoods. Those same neighborhoods have the poorest access to health care; the worst public transportation to reach a good hospital; and the highest absenteeism rate in local high schools because the children are experiencing asthma.

The same story repeats, across categories of inequity, for so many issues. Redlining in the early 1900s subjected entire geographic zones of our
city to low property values and low mortgage access. Disproportionately, in
2023, Black city residents in these very same zones have significantly lower
housing equity, significantly higher rental costs, and high rates of mortgage
denial. They have high debt loads with partial college completion, and their
credit scores, in turn, cause automated mortgage AI software to deny their
applications. Yet they pay rental costs that exceed what a monthly mortgage
would have cost—and they do so with seasonal income that is variable and,
therefore, unqualifiable for the mortgage lenders. They spend more money
and earn less home equity than all other city residents.

And for those few who do own homes in formerly redlined zones? We
can show that, house by house, their homes' assessed values overestimate
the true sales prices they can achieve by the greatest margins, whereas afflu-
ent districts in Pittsburgh have the largest underestimates of assessed values
compared to sales prices. And so, with one of the nation's highest property
tax rates, our city massively overcharges the poorest residents and under-
charges the richest at the very same time.

Heinz helped fund the CREATE Lab to show such inequities in undeniable detail, and I knew that their fundamental concern was not research
for research's sake, but rather authentically dismantling the inequities that
are drowning our region's residents. So, I responded, almost instantly, that
Heinz did not want to fund yet another research center. They would want
us to reshape the university's practices so that we could all directly engage
with the community to dismantle structural barriers to equity in our region.
Heinz would want us to stop scaling up, thinking globally, and instead scale
down and recognize our moral responsibility to the local neighborhood.

I expected a blue-sky response this unconventional to fail rhetorically—
after all, a university's fundamental mission is twofold: education and research. Moral responsibility to the local community is not there at the
highest level of visibility. But instead of demurral, I was absolutely stunned
to receive support and encouragement from everyone—from the president,
the trustees, the deans, and, eventually, the Heinz trustees and staff.

Acknowledging institutional moral responsibility is a high hill to climb. Accepting that the incentive structures and capacities of the university can really change so that every member of campus feels supported in doing community-engaged equity work as part of their identity—that is like scaling Everest.

We considered program design for two years, working internally at Carnegie Mellon, and visiting several times with the foundation's leadership. One early, and very exciting, conclusion we reached was that the attention we would turn to local equity must be permanent. One cannot do equity work and then stop, because the grotesque incentive structures in systems of power and capital will just slide the community back towards inequity again. So, we all agreed: we need a permanent, endowed center that outlives us all: a Center for Shared Prosperity.

Architects know the joy of this—the weight and excitement of designing a cultural transformation that is value-based and designed to outlast the authors—which gave me a sense of purpose and internal reward beyond anything I had felt before. Answering the question of where to even begin, over the first few years, was also the hardest challenge I have faced.

Our initial design for how the Center would operate was based on three basic theories of change. First, everyone needs permission to do the good work. Incentive structures throughout the university need to allow, encourage and reward community engagement and equity work, just as they reward research and education today—the classical pillars of a university's mission. But this requires small and large internal, organizational changes at the college that can shift the culture of permissible work over the course of years.

We have had to design systems for staff to effectively obtain permission to spend work time in community efforts; ways for faculty to boast about their equity work during their tenure review; annual review procedures where supervisors can listen to staff describe their community work, congratulate them, and make that work part of their case for promotion. We have designed funded internship programs for students to spend their summers engaging with community organizations while being paid a living wage. We created a university-wide award recognition program so that deans would have the yearly ritual of meeting staff who have done outstanding community work—elevating the voice of the staff and creating opportunities for them to interact with university leadership regularly. The list of changes goes on, and all these small organizational modifications need to add up to a sea change in attitude: the university as a place where interconnection with community is essential to our identity.

The second fundamental need we recognized was that of capacity. Some colleges have deep engagements with community already—architecture students frequently spend time in communities, studying and co-designing improvements to the urban landscape; but many colleges do not have such customs. What's more, when we talk to communities throughout Pittsburgh, we hear the same story that you will confront in every urban setting: sometimes the university does research *on* us and then leaves—we spend our valuable time with them, uncompensated, and when they leave, we are left with literally nothing to show from the interaction. We are just being used.

With the best of intentions, universities can enter a community, claiming to know what the community needs—claiming the mantle of wisdom and talent. These power plays result in communities that turn allergic to academic work, impeding even well-intentioned academics from meaningfully connecting.

I ran into many community leaders who said, "No, we refuse to work with you ever again." The examples are too numerous to be taken as the odd exception; and the fundamental sin that they display is that of the university devaluing the community and its residents, mistaking their marginalization for lack of wisdom and lack of know-how.

The structural barriers that have made these communities poor and low-resourced are the fault of unjust privilege. The neighborhoods of Pittsburgh are vibrant because of the strength, wisdom, and tenacity of residents who invest incredible resources into helping their neighborhoods despite the historical disadvantage meted to them from those in power.

Lack of capacity means a chronic shortage of the understanding of our privileged relationship to the community. What is the history of inequitable treatment that the university has participated in shaping? What is the history of marginalization that has resulted in dramatically different life outcomes in specific neighborhoods, spanning pollution, redlining, health mis-care, mortgage denial? And how do faculty, staff, and students from a university engage as peers with community members—co-discovering solutions to structural challenges? What rituals must be part of a peer-based engagement—like honoraria for every community member whenever we ask them to give us their time?

It is not enough to create the context of permission for college members to do community work; we also have to prepare them to do such work without causing harm. It is a large-scale, multi-year professional development challenge that needs just as many faceted techniques within the institution as the organizational changes needed for incentive alignment.

It turns out these first two challenges are largely social. We have to win over every part of the university administration, student groups, independent faculty—and we have to convince them that there is learning to be had and changes to be made in how we function. All of this has to succeed without making them feel defensive and without making the challenges feel insurmountable. So—honest acknowledgement of injustice has to be combined with an authentic sense of hope in a delicate balance, and this means the ground team must be truly amazing to do all this across the departmental boundaries of an institution with more than ten thousand members.

The third challenge extends beyond the university and its inside-work, recognizing the fact that if we want the university to have real impact on inequity in Pittsburgh, then we must forge a permanent, wholesome, peer-based relationship with residents and community organizations. To reach parts of the community that we did not already know, we used a nomination process, asking our friends throughout the region to suggest colleagues for an inaugural Center Community Committee, C3.

The past three years, interacting with C3 and watching them identify and launch projects has been eye-opening along every dimension.

C3 members tell us about services that existed in Pittsburgh—like strong community centers that were loving and caring places in their youth—that have disappeared over the years due to lack of funding. Countless C3 members and community residents they know do the hard work of battling against injustice, with zero cash and with little personal economic cushion: book lending programs for incarcerated individuals, eyeglass programs, financial fluency work, voting drives, air pollution action, food deliveries in nutritional deserts.

Marginalization has not created islands of hopelessness; instead, it has catalyzed powerful action—particularly by Black women in Pittsburgh, fighting every headwind you can imagine to defend the lives of their children, the elderly, and everyone in between. Religious intensity in our community members bridges *between* religions—with Black leaders who are Muslim and Christian working fiercely together on local issues.

I learned early that the respect we owe our residents drills all the way to greetings. I say "Miss Terri" and "Miss Elaine," "Mama C" and "Mama Ayana." Kinship, respect, and a thick-skinned refusal to bow under pressure are the hallmarks I see; in contrast, my own university populace feels wishy-washy and easily wilted—a privilege available only to those with power and capital.

More than a dozen never-ending programs have been launched by C3, funding community organizations and students at CMU to create programs that have structural influence on our region. One example is Colorful Backgrounds, a program run by two community organizations that take the very best from past, defunded post-incarceration service programs and combine them to create a winning model: expungement services, financial training, interview coaching, healing circles, career planning, and more.

I went to a Unitarian neighborhood church and witnessed the graduation ceremony for one of the first-year classes. Watching the pride shared between formerly incarcerated persons and their families—all out in force that day, in the splendor of graduation gowns—the mood was exhilarating. To be truly systemic, the training program also provides a full introduction to political advocacy—because no one is better positioned to advocate for carceral reform than these women and men who have personally experienced the carceral system and its degradations. Prior post-carceral programs ran their course then closed down when funders tired of repeatedly funding the same program—this is the uncanny way in which foundations heal and harm the same communities, time and again. But for Colorful Backgrounds, the Center for Shared Prosperity is dedicated to finding sustained funds so the program can continue nonstop. Temporary is not an option in equity work.

Another example of a C3 program is Nourishing Neighborhood Safety. This program builds a counter-narrative to the concept that neighborhood safety is improved by pouring more money into policing. Instead, NNS is funding three individuals who already pursued meaningful neighborhood programs, each in their own place, each with the cultural knowledge to design a truly effective local intervention. All three were unfunded volunteers, scraping together their own money and small donations to pay for books, transportation, and support. CSP has a chance to fund at scale and to document just how the work provides local benefits, so that the efficacy of such locally funded action becomes undeniable to policymakers.

When we have meetings with updates on these neighborhoods' programs, we end up shedding tears on the call. An organizer talks about the one person who believed in her and provided her first resources, and how that has now grown to a support network that is changing lives. She will become emotional, then all of us join in because the stories are so deeply fundamental to identity, equity, justice. Nothing in the conversation is frill and superficial; nothing about the work is optional.

The Center work is at its early stages—just two years in—and it will consume my efforts until I retire; I made this promise to Heinz and to CMU at the outset. I already see, through this left turn, a career pivot that helps me exploit a position of privilege—my tenure, my funding connections, my entire university—for a part in effecting the kinds of systemic changes that are the moral obligations that we all share.

GigaPan connected me to scientists across the world; it nurtured the joy of interdisciplinary science and forged for me a network of connections to scientists who adore their work every day. The Center for Shared Prosperity has given me a place in a new social network, one that gifts me with the ability to adore the work every day with the same passion that I saw twenty years ago in scientists and photographers worldwide.

Now I think I might know where I belong. I belong in the middle of justice-oriented work. I belong between community and privilege, as a connector that squeezes the best possible value out of privilege in the service of justice. I belong on the level, affording power and agency to the community, showing my colleagues how we can lower our standing by raising the stage of others and fighting against the oppression of hierarchy and the transaction of power.

Finding this particular place to occupy has taken a lifetime, because it is a concatenation of experiences that give substance to identity—being Iranian and Muslim; witnessing bigotry personally; feeling safer among the marginalized; learning to act against an unjust war; aligning innovation with ethics; collecting the privilege that I can now spend. But the nature of this place, this form of belonging, is ultimately for me to sit between groups—to belong in the intermediating space.

Coda

SFO

My children were young, six and eight, when we visited family in San Francisco and then found ourselves at the new United Airlines gates waiting for the redeye flight to Pittsburgh. I had enjoyed showing my children around my old haunts, including my favorite fish and chips spot in Princeton-by-the-Sea, near Half Moon Bay, and a picnic in the Rodin sculpture garden at Stanford.

The United terminal was just refurbished, with strong white lights, an angled ceiling at least three stories high, and plentiful seating, all of it arranged in facing rows, and all of it entirely packed with passengers. My children and I sat in one seating row, with me in the middle, facing another row of chairs less than six feet in front of us. Beyond that row, we could see the giant picture windows facing the night sky where our Boeing would park along the jet bridge.

I was mostly consumed with all the regular, hyperactive interactions with my children, but noticed early on that an older gentleman was sitting in the bank of chairs facing us and staring intently at me, most particularly at how I was interacting with my daughter. In the way that one becomes more and more uncomfortable with a social situation that is out of control, I would glance more often in his direction and began to feel my anxiety rising. He was staring very obviously, and his face suggested that he was becoming more and more upset with something he saw in how I talked and gestured with my daughter.

We were easily half an hour or more from boarding, and this was not getting any better. His face hardened further, and he started talking. The words were imperceptible at first, just a muttering, but he gradually became loud enough for me to hear his words: "I'm gonna kill you." As I began to make out the words, other passengers sitting around him became aware of the situation as well.

I looked in the direction of the United gate kiosk, but no agent had arrived yet. I wanted to find someone to ask for help, but I also could not imagine leaving my children alone there, even for five seconds. Conversations around us died down because many were feeling the discomfort of the situation. I was scared, because he was staring at me intently. But my fear morphed into extreme concern for my children's safety.

We had backpacks and books sprawled on the chairs and floor. Do we pack up? Do we just run away, toward the back of the area? Retreat did not seem useful or particularly safe in the situation, and so we stayed seated, with my children entirely, and thankfully, unaware of the entire scene even as it unfolded.

If you are a parent, there is a wild kingdom version of this that you have surely experienced. You are sitting somewhere on the ground with your child. And some natural danger appears before you. A yellow jacket is circling, or a menacing spider is sitting on the ground right next to your son. Our flight reflexes, when family is in danger, melt away. I have done things I would never, normally, have the courage to do—like swat the spider, palm down, and crush it immediately, because my son was *right there*.

So in the moment, with no obvious help available from airline personnel, I did something I cannot totally justify and never would have predicted. I stood up, walked over with my hand outstretched to the gentleman, ensuring that I was between him and my children. I introduced myself.

"Hi. I'm Illah. We're going to Pittsburgh. How are you?"

He shook my hand as if we were at a business meeting, seated, and it was as if a switch flipped completely. He said hello back, we talked about the redeye flight briefly, then he wished me a good flight and that was that.

Later, during boarding, a woman in line came up to me and asked me how I did that. She said she was frozen, too, watching him grow angry and loud. She had watched him looking at me with fury, and she saw me walking over, never imagining that the man's anger would just evaporate. She asked me what in heavens I said to him, and what could possibly have moved me to take that risk. We talked about children and spiders.

How we respond in moments of crisis is just a reflection of everything we have experienced, so far. It is more automatic and reflexive than rational or premeditated. This particular episode reminds me always of two aspects of our human journey. First, how we behave is truly impossible to predict ahead of time. But, with distance and perspective, we can usually see that who we have become inspires how we behave. Second, caring human interaction is the only path that makes any sense. That will never change.

I am preparing for a series of international meetings as I write these words; there is a UN General Assembly meeting, a World Economic Forum meeting, and more. The conveners are busy announcing, in so many words, that the world has become multipolar and that the United States has become ineffective. The fractiousness we constantly talk about is dislocating all of us from belonging to a coherent, empathetic story. We all have to strive for connection, and I believe it is only through that effort that we can each identify our own personal place of belonging.

Acknowledgments

This work would never have matured into something worth publishing without my readers. They engaged with early drafts and provided the constant, honest feedback I needed throughout the revision process. Ted Koppel pushed me to always rewrite for the audience. He championed the right beginning for this book. Mitra Nourbakhsh gave me the confidence that the road I was following was true. Michael Genesereth inspired the best ending for the book.

A memoir of lived experience is built upon the care of all the family that have surrounded me: my relatives, my children, Nikou and Mitra, my life partner, Jen. You all have given me the love and patience to take on a task this personal, and to see it to its conclusion.

The career I describe in this work has been a hyper-social one, built upon consistent team efforts, each project a decade in the making. For their willingness to trust me, to believe in me and to devote so much of their career trajectories to our collaboration, I will forever be in the debt of all my research groups: the Mobile Robot Programming Lab, the CREATE Lab, the NASA Intelligent Robotics Group, and the Center for Shared Prosperity. To more than one hundred colleagues who have been critical to my life's work: our successes have been defined by your generosity and your values. I will always appreciate you.

Next, I want to turn to Sentient Publications, the press that has been generous enough to take on this project of mine. Publishers both greatly improve the author's work and also lend the legitimacy that is so very important in our noisy digital age. I especially want to thank Deborah Weisser and Marissa Cassayre. Their keen eyes have played a formative role in shaping this book into something worth reading.

Index

About Sentient Publications

Founded in 2001, Sentient Publications is an independent publisher of nonfiction books on transformative spirituality, cultural creativity, holistic health, new science, and beyond.

Our authors are intensely interested in exploring the nature of reality from fresh perspectives, addressing life's great questions, and fostering the full expression of human potential. Our books arise from the spirit of inquiry and the richness of the inherent dialogue between writer and reader. We strive to release books into the world that will uplift and empower readers in both their inner and outer lives.

Independent publishers want and need your support. If you have comments, questions, or would like to connect with us, feel free to reach out.

SENTIENT PUBLICATIONS
A Limited Liability Company
PO Box 1851
Boulder, CO 80306
www.sentientpublications.com